COOKING
WITH
MRS SIMKINS

COOKING
WITH
MRS SIMKINS

HOW TO COOK SIMPLE, WHOLESOME, HOME-MADE MEALS

SPRING HILL

In loving memory of my Mum and Dad,
Pam and Ron

Published by Spring Hill, an imprint of How To Books Ltd.
Spring Hill House, Spring Hill Road
Begbroke, Oxford OX5 1RX
United Kingdom
Tel: (01865) 375794
Fax: (01865) 379162
info@howtobooks.co.uk
www.howtobooks.co.uk

How To Books greatly reduce the carbon footprint of their bo
by sourcing their typesetting and printing in the UK.

The paper used for this book is FSC certified and totally chlorine-free. FSC (The Forest Stewardship
Council) is an international network to promote responsible management of the world's forests.

Text © 2010 Mrs Simkins
British Library Cataloguing in Publication Data
A catalogue record of this book is available from the British Library.

ISBN: 978-1-905862-36-8

Produced for How To Books by Deer Park Productions, Tavistock, Devon
Designed and typeset by Mousemat Design Ltd
Printed and bound in Great Britain by Cromwell Press Group, Trowbridge, Wiltshire

NOTE: The material contained in this book is set out in good faith for general guidance and no
liability can be accepted for loss or expense incurred as a result of relying in particular circumstances
on statements made in the book. Laws and regulations are complex and liable to change, and readers
should check the current position with relevant authorities before making personal arrangements.

CONTENTS

Acknowledgements

I would like to thank my family and friends and everyone who helped with the making of this book.

Special thanks to Beryl Cooke, Nicola Tarling and Sophie Pender-Cudlip.

Thank you to Fanny Charles and everyone at the *Blackmore Vale* Magazine, and to all at the *Messenger*.

Finally, a huge thank you to everyone at How To Books.

Thank you all very much indeed.

INTRODUCTION

Cooking for yourself and eating well

I first made the connection between eating well and cooking for yourself while enduring school dinners in primary school. The food was, unfortunately, *completely horrible and disgusting* and not at all like the food at home. After quite a long time I realised the dry leathery stuff with silvery lines of gristle running through it was actually roast beef and the thin brown liquid with the peculiar dusty smell was in fact gravy. We didn't have beef at home very often but when we did, it was a delicious treat. Mum's gravy was rich and smooth and Dad's creamy, fluffy mashed potato absolutely *never* had scary little grey lumps in it.

Clearly, to eat well, you needed to be able to cook.

Good kitchen practice

Good hygiene is essential in the kitchen: keep all surfaces and equipment scrupulously clean, change cleaning cloths and tea towels daily.

Always wash hands before cooking and always after handling raw meat, raw fish and raw eggs and their shells. Be sure to wash surfaces and equipment that have come into contact with any of these with hot water and detergent.

Wash any fruit or vegetable that is to be eaten raw. There is a common misconception that there is no need to wash organic produce; it is very necessary though, as a major reason for washing fruit and vegetables is to wash away any bacteria.

Store all meat, fish, dairy products and eggs in the fridge. Keep raw meat and fish covered and on the lowest shelf, where it is colder. Rather than store raw meat and fish in its wrapping alone, keep in a dish or container to avoid any fluids seeping out into the fridge and contaminating other foods.

Cool any cooked foods quickly before storing in the fridge: otherwise they can raise the temperature of the fridge to unsafe levels. If you need to cover food while it is cooling, do so only loosely: greaseproof paper is ideal, or a loose covering of foil. Never leave cooked food, particularly meat, sitting around in a warm room for any length of time.

Be sure all food is as fresh as possible. Chicken, turkey and pork should always be cooked through completely. If reheating food be sure it is piping hot throughout and only reheat food once.

Thaw frozen food in the fridge if possible. If you defrost food in the microwave cook it as soon as it has defrosted.

Clean the inside of the fridge every week, deal with anything suspicious lurking at the back and mop up any overlooked nasty stains. If you are buying fresh supplies of foodstuffs you have in stock already, be sure to use everything in date order.

Oven temperature conversions

Mark 1	275°F	140°C
Mark 2	300°F	150°C
Mark 3	325°F	170°C
Mark 4	350°F	180°C
Mark 5	375°F	190°C
Mark 6	400°F	200°C
Mark 7	425°F	220°C
Mark 8	450°F	230°C

Please be aware that individual oven performance varies tremendously.

Measurements

Both metric and imperial measurements are given for the recipes. Follow one set of measurements only for each recipe, not a mixture of both, as they are not interchangeable.

Where ingredients are largely available in metric weights only, such as tinned goods and cartons of cream, the metric weights only have been given.

Helpful equipment

Here are some suggestions for a few tools and bits and pieces that are useful to have. This is not a guide to everything you need to equip the kitchen: it is more a list of extra items you might not think of that can be very helpful for specific tasks. In addition to the list below, it is also useful to have a food processor, microwave and bread machine.

Apple corer

An apple corer is very handy for preparing apples for cooking. The plastic tube-like ones with a plunger are especially convenient. Apple corers are much more accurate and safe than the point of a peeler.

Burger press

If you make burgers quite often it is worth buying an inexpensive plastic burger press. They can look a bit flimsy but they are surprisingly robust, last for years, and make good firm burgers.

Ceramic baking beans

Ceramic baking beans conduct the heat more efficiently than dried peas or beans when baking pastry flan cases blind. They help to conduct heat to the inside of the pastry case as well as weighing it down.

Cooling racks
A cooling rack is a must for cooling cakes and biscuits. If you don't have one, you can use a clean grill rack instead.

Domed mesh food covers
These are essential during the summer to protect food from flies and very good indeed if you are eating in the garden. They are also useful to protect cooling bread and cakes during the fly season.

Flexible rubber or plastic spatulas
These are extremely useful for scraping the last drop from mixing bowls and for scraping the mixture down from the sides of your food processor bowl.

Grapefruit knife
The slightly curved and double-edged blade is the ideal tool for separating grapefruit segments.

Greaseproof paper
This is essential for wrapping round cakes to stop them from burning on top, loosely covering baking that has just come out of the oven, or loosely covering proving bread and pizza dough. You also need it to wrap cakes and Christmas puddings that need to be stored for a while.

Heatproof litre (or quart) measuring jug
This is very useful for measuring, mixing, and cooking in the microwave.

Heavy-bottomed milk saucepan
A good-quality heavy-gauge saucepan is essential for milk-based sauces and custards which will burn in anything too thin.

Lemon reamer
A simple wooden lemon reamer is a quick and easy way to juice a small number of citrus fruits, although in an emergency a dinner fork can work surprisingly well.

Lemon zester
A lemon zester is the best tool for zesting a small amount of citrus fruit. If you have quite a lot of fruit to zest a microplane grater would be better. Microplanes make lovely fluffy finely grated cheese as well. There is no need to spend a fortune on these, a simple all stainless steel one is more than adequate.

Oven thermometer
It is useful to be able to check the accuracy of your oven temperature dial.

Palette knives

A small palette knife is essential for lifting biscuits from the baking tray, lifting uncooked biscuits on to the tray, loosening cakes and pastries from baking tins, spreading icing and buttercream and so on. A large palette knife doesn't have quite so many uses but it's difficult to loosen cakes from the bottom of a loose-bottomed cake tin properly without one.

Pastry brush

If you are going to make bread and pastry fairly often and need to glaze the top with milk or egg wash, it's difficult to manage without a brush. A pure bristle one, rather than nylon, is also useful for brushing the pan with oil when making pancakes and Welsh cakes.

Plastic picnic knife

If you can get hold of some of those quite strong and robust plastic picnic knives – the kind that come in a set with spoons and forks and have a serrated edge – they are very handy for cutting through shortbread and brownies and so on, as they won't scratch the surface of your baking tins. They are also ideal for slicing lettuce without browning the cut edge.

Plastic spaghetti server

Spaghetti is quite tricky to serve without one of these and they are also handy for lowering eggs into boiling water and getting them out again. A simple plastic one works best.

Potato ricer

A potato ricer makes beautifully fluffy mashed potatoes. Even if you use a dinner fork to mash your potatoes most of the time it is worth taking the extra trouble for special occasions.

Rotary food mill

You will find this ideal for making smooth soups and puréeing baby food.

Screw-top jar with plastic lid

A glass jar with a plastic lid, such as the ones that peanut butter comes in, is perfect for shaking up a quick salad dressing.

Sea salt mill

If you prefer to use less salt in your cooking, it's nice to use smaller amounts of a well-flavoured sea salt such as Maldon Salt. You can buy salt mills especially for grinding sea salt flakes which is handy if you need a finer texture for a particular dish.

Spatter guards

These are great for preventing splashes of oil or tomato sauce or curry from getting everywhere in the vicinity of the hob. You can get very cheap ones but they don't last very long at all: a good-quality one made of stainless steel is more efficient and better value.

Swivel vegetable peeler
A swivel peeler – the narrow kind you hold like a knife – makes short work of peeling potatoes and other vegetables and is also useful for peeling shavings of citrus peel or hard cheeses such as Parmesan.

Tablespoons, teaspoons, dessertspoons, dinner knives and forks
Tablespoons are a standard kitchen measure, as are teaspoons, and dessertspoons to a lesser degree. Dinner knives are ideal for mixing scone dough and dinner forks are perfect for lightly beating eggs, mashing potatoes and other vegetables, pricking shortbread and pastry cases and raising ridges on mashed potato topped pies.

Tea strainer
A tea strainer is useful for sieving small amounts of lemon juice, or used with a teaspoon, it's great for dusting flour or icing sugar over bread and cakes.

Wobbly whisk
A more correct name for this is 'bedspring coil whisk' and that tells you all you need to know about its appearance! These have the best action for whisking pancake and Yorkshire pudding batter.

Baking Tins
You don't need to clutter up your cupboards with every size of baking tin. These are the most useful sizes. Heavier, better quality baking tins conduct heat more efficiently than anything thin and flimsy: they also have a longer life.

Large baking tray
A baking tray that just fits comfortably inside your oven can be used for all kinds of bread and biscuits and scones.

Standard 20cm (8in) square brownie tin
This is a really useful size and shape for brownies and small tray bakes.

12-cup muffin tin
As well as muffins this is perfect for buns, rolls, fairy cakes and deep filled tarts.

12-cup tart tins
It's useful to have a couple of these for tarts, mince pies, small quiches and for steadying crispy cakes.

Loose-bottomed cake, sandwich and flan tins

It's handy to have the following sizes:

18cm (7in) cake tin; Pair of 18cm (7in) sandwich tins; 20cm (8in) cake tin; 20cm (8in) flan tin; 23cm (9in) cake tin – particularly if you make your own Christmas cake.

Large and small roasting tins

A small roasting tin is useful for small joints and cuts of meat, roast potatoes and other roast vegetables, large Yorkshire puddings and small batches of buns and rolls. A large roasting tin is useful for large joints of meat and turkey.

BREAKFASTS

The majority of recipes and 'serving suggestions' in this section are intended for weekends and holidays, and when guests are staying, rather than for the average weekday morning.

See also **Very Quick Light Meals on Toast** for more egg dishes.

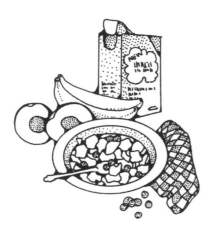

THE FULL ENGLISH

This is such a popular meal you see signs for 'the all day breakfast' everywhere you go. In fact, it's probably better not to try to tackle something like this first thing in the morning. Possibly, a large cooked breakfast was never intended to be eaten the very moment you got up. Farm workers would have been up at first light milking the cows and tending the animals and only tucking in to a hearty 'farmhouse' breakfast after half a morning's hard physical work. The landed gentry would probably have been up for a while as well, having enjoyed their early morning tea and freshly ironed newspapers in bed!

As with a roast dinner, many people seem to be under the impression that a cooked breakfast is child's play to prepare. Just like the roast dinner it *is* straightforward but there are quite a few elements that need strict organisation to bring everything to the table at the same time.

Instead of tackling the complete full English, sometimes you might prefer to serve just a couple of elements together such as: bacon and egg, or bacon and mushrooms, possibly bacon, tomatoes and fried slice (fried bread), and so on. Fried slice and baked beans is especially popular with children.

Action Plan for the Full English Breakfast

First of all, decide which of the various components you are going to have. Choose from: bacon, eggs, sausages, mushrooms, tomatoes, fried slice, fried potatoes, black pudding, baked beans and fried potatoes. Next, try to organise somewhere to keep the plates nice and warm, as most parts of a cooked breakfast can get cold really easily. Of course, you can use the grill as well, but in practice it is difficult to monitor with so many things going on at the same time and if fat splashes over the element the atmosphere in the kitchen can get a bit acrid and unpleasant!

If you are having **Sausages**, it is much easier to cook them in the oven: they will cook beautifully, they will be off your mind for most of the 20 minutes or so they take to cook, and they won't be taking up room on the hob. See **Sausages and Mash** in the **Main Meals** section for full instructions.

If you are having **Fried Potatoes**, start them at the same time as the sausages as they take a similar time to cook. See below for full instructions.

Mushrooms can go on next: they only take a few minutes to cook but can be kept warm without spoiling. You might choose closed cap, button or chestnut but the larger ones with the open gills are tastier and more traditional. Bear in mind though, if you choose the open variety they will stain everything they come into contact with a murky black! Heat some oil in a pan and cook the mushrooms over a moderate heat: put a lid on the pan so that the mushrooms half fry, half steam until they are soft and succulent.

Tomatoes, cut in halves, are the next to go in. If you have a large enough pan and they can go in with the bacon: it will give them a lovely flavour. Otherwise, they can cook in a pan of their own, or, if you are short of space, bake them in a lightly oiled dish in the oven while the sausages are cooking. Don't forget to turn them halfway through the cooking time.

Bacon: back bacon is a good breakfast bacon although lovers of crispy bacon might prefer streaky.

Fry the bacon in a very lightly oiled pan over a moderate heat, turning from time to time until it is cooked to your liking. **Black pudding** can cook at the same time. Try to get a really decent one from the butcher and avoid anything plastic wrapped.

Fried slice: if you have time and space to keep the bacon warm for a while, fried bread cooked in bacon fat has a lovely flavour. Otherwise, heat some oil, not too much, in a pan over a moderately hot heat, put in your bread (triangles look appetising), cook briefly on both sides, turn down the heat to moderate and fry until dry and crisp. You might like to spread a little Marmite on the bread very lightly before you fry it.

If you are having **baked beans**, put them on to heat now. They can be cooked in the microwave if the hob is full.

Fried eggs: these need to be cooked last of all in a clean pan and served immediately. Heat some oil and turn the heat down to moderate just before you put the eggs in. Keep the pan moderately hot but not excessively so. Unless your pan is extra large, four eggs are realistically the most you can fry at one time.

Sunny side up: this usually means a set white and a runny yolk. To make sure that the yolk is hot all the way through, put a lid on the pan for a few moments. Alternatively, if there is enough oil in the bottom of the pan you can baste the egg very carefully with the hot oil, using a spoon.

Over easy: this is more of an American diner term and means the egg has been flipped over briefly and back again. This has the effect of giving the yolk a nice opaque pink tinge.

Crispy bottom: you might like your fried egg to have a crispy, lacy bottom: if you do, you need to keep the heat high, but be aware that the bottom of the yolk can go hard when you do this.

Fried apple: something else you might like to try if you are having sausages and/or black pudding is fried apple. If you haven't had it before, it may sound strange but it is absolutely lovely. Core the apple (there is no need to peel it unless you want to) and cut it into wedges or rings. Fry gently in a little butter and a splash of oil until soft and just starting to caramelise around the edges. Fried apple is also good with sausages and mash or pork chops.

Don't forget the toast and marmalade, brown sauce, and possibly tomato ketchup and mustard.

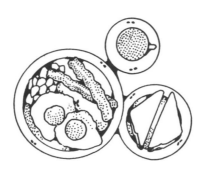

FRIED POTATOES

Simple home fried potatoes are absolutely lovely. My Mum used to tell me about staying with farming relatives when she was a small child: the farm workers would come in from the fields for their breakfast, ravenously hungry, and tuck in to huge great mounds of golden fried potatoes; nothing else, just fried potatoes and big mugs of tea!

To achieve the proper taste and texture it is essential to boil the potatoes first and they must be cold when you slice them. Although you can use any kind of potato, new potatoes are particularly good and there is no need to peel them. This is also a great way to use up leftover potatoes. See **Leftovers** in the **Roast Dinners** section.

Quantity of potatoes to suit
Oil for frying
A little salt to serve

Prepare and boil the potatoes. Leave to cool completely. Slice into thicknesses of a little less than a centimetre. Heat a little oil in a wide, shallow pan and fry on both sides until golden. Drain on kitchen paper and serve immediately.

BACON SANDWICH

A bacon sandwich is possibly even closer to the nation's heart than the full English breakfast. Some people maintain that a proper bacon sandwich should be made with wrapped thin-sliced white bread but many agree that the best bacon sandwiches are made with fairly thick slices from a decent uncut white loaf. Other areas for debate are: buttered or plain bread? Brown sauce or tomato ketchup? A fringe element might suggest a touch of mustard or even pickle (very nice indeed, actually!).

Whichever way is your favourite, fry your bacon as above: back bacon makes a lovely satisfying sandwich but for crispy fans, streaky works well.

BACON, EGG AND MUSHROOM SANDWICH

This is virtually a complete fried breakfast between two slices of bread. Prepare the bacon, eggs and mushrooms as above. Again, white bread from a decent uncut loaf works well.

FRIED EGG SANDWICH

Your true friends must be those you don't mind sitting down and eating a fried egg sandwich with! Fry two eggs per sandwich until the white is set but the yolks are still runny. Lift the eggs onto a slice of buttered bread, season with freshly ground black pepper, possibly a touch of salt, and cover with another slice. Squash down so that the yolk runs into the bread, and cut into two.

HAM AND EGG IN A MUFFIN

The muffin referred to here is the round, flat bread type one that the old Muffin Man in the nursery rhyme used to sell, now known as an 'English muffin'. You can either poach or fry the eggs. If you are frying, those special rings you can buy to make a fried egg perfectly round add a nice touch.

For each person: lightly toast and butter a muffin, cover the bottom with a slice of ham or make a little pile of wafer thin ham, cover with a poached or fried egg and put the muffin lid on top.

You can use fried or grilled bacon instead of ham if you prefer. Incidentally, a couple of poached eggs served on the two halves of a lightly toasted and buttered muffin are soothing and delicious for breakfast, lunch or supper.

KIPPERS AND SMOKED HADDOCK

Kippers (a whole herring split, opened out and cold smoked) and smoked haddock both make a lovely breakfast served with a poached egg and brown bread and butter. Kippers are an oily fish and smoked haddock is a smoked white fish. Kippers have a deep, rich flavour and smoked haddock is more delicate. Both seem to be enhanced by a cup of tea and by finishing up any leftover bread and butter with marmalade.

The cooking method given below, using a closely fitting lid, minimises any smell.

SMOKED HADDOCK

There are several ways to cook smoked haddock including poaching in milk or water. This is a simple and straightforward method to cook a smoked fillet of haddock. Put a very little oil and/or butter in a frying pan, add the haddock and cover with a closely fitting lid. Cook the haddock over a moderate heat for a few minutes until the fish loses its translucency and becomes opaque: usually about 10–12 minutes. You may like to rest a bay leaf on top of the fish as it cooks.

Serve on warmed plates with lightly poached eggs, a good grinding of freshly ground black pepper and brown bread and butter.

KIPPERS

Kippers are very reasonably priced: you can buy kipper fillets, whole boned kippers, or whole kippers. Whole kippers with the bone in are generally acknowledged to have the best flavour but the boned kippers are good and suitable for those who would prefer to avoid fish bones (although there may still be the odd stray bone). Kipper fillets, although still beautifully flavoured, are on the whole more popular with the less dedicated kipper enthusiast.

As with smoked haddock above, cook in a lightly oiled frying pan, with a closely fitting lid over a moderate heat until cooked through: usually 5–10 minutes. Serve as above.

What is the difference between cold smoked and hot smoked?

If something is hot smoked it is actually cooked during the smoking process and you don't need to cook it further (although you can, if you like). If something is cold smoked, it is well flavoured and has had its keeping qualities prolonged but it is still actually raw, and you will need to cook it. A Finnan haddock, for example (a whole haddock, split and opened out) is cold smoked, but an Arbroath smokie (a whole haddock, cleaned but not opened out) is hot smoked. Also, the genuine articles are never artificially coloured with liquid smoke. A smoked haddock fillet is a boneless slice or side of haddock and has been cold smoked: try to buy undyed if you can, there is a world of difference.

To add to the confusion, smoked salmon is usually cold smoked, but has first been either cured in dry salt or brine, and so doesn't need further cooking. Having said that, salmon may also be hot smoked.

Kedgeree: see page 48

Simple Fish Cakes: see page 42

TOASTED BAGELS WITH SMOKED SALMON AND CREAM CHEESE

This is a lovely treat to have over the Christmas holidays (several times, if possible!)

1–2 bagels per person Cream cheese Slices of smoked salmon	Split and *lightly* toast the bagels and spread with cream cheese. Arrange slices of smoked salmon on top.
Black pepper and wedges of lemon	Serve with wedges of lemon and freshly ground black pepper. A glass of champagne as well would be just perfect.

Scrambled Eggs with Smoked Salmon: see page 134

Porridge and Oatmeal

Porridge and oatmeal differ in that porridge is made from whole oats that have been crushed or rolled, and oatmeal is made from oats that have been milled to produce a kind of coarse flour. Porridge is made by stirring water and porridge oats together and cooking them together, whereas with oatmeal you stir the oatmeal gradually into already boiling water. Oatmeal is always made with water whereas porridge can be made with all water, all milk, or half and half. Porridge has a creamy, soothing flavour, oatmeal tastes sharper and nuttier. Both are nutritious ways to start the day.

Porridge
Per serving

It's easier to measure porridge in a cup or mug: as a rough guide use 1 part oats to 2 parts liquid, which can be cold milk or water or half and half.

Stir the oats and liquid together in a heavy-bottomed saucepan and bring to the boil. Turn the heat down and simmer for a minimum of three minutes (depending on how large an amount you are making), stirring constantly.

Serve with a little brown sugar or honey and maybe a spot of thin cream on special occasions. Alternatively, put a few raisins or dried cranberries in the bottom of your serving bowl and pour the porridge on top: they will plump up nicely in the heat from the porridge. You can add a little salt to taste if you prefer.

You can also make good porridge in the microwave (see the manufacturer's instructions) but it can be quite prone to boiling over.

Oatmeal
Oatmeal really does need a little salt: not too much, just a small pinch per serving.

Per serving

Bring **275ml (½ pint) water** to the boil in a heavy-bottomed saucepan and sprinkle in **40g (1½oz) oatmeal**, stirring constantly as you do so. Turn down the heat and simmer for about 5 minutes, stirring all the time. Leave to stand for a few moments before serving. Add **a little salt** to taste.

It can be easier to make oatmeal for one in the microwave. Keep an eye on it as it can soon boil over. **Pour 275ml (½ pint) boiling water** into a large heatproof jug and sprinkle in **40g (1½ oz) oatmeal**, stirring as you do so. Microwave on High for 1–2 minutes, depending on your microwave, as it can boil over quickly. Stir thoroughly and stand for a few moments. Return to the microwave for a further half minute to a minute. Stir again and leave to stand for a few moments before serving. Add **salt to taste.**

Serve with a little brown sugar or honey and maybe a spot of thin cream on special occasions.

40g of oatmeal roughly equates to 2 heaped tablespoons.

Using a spurtle

A spurtle (a stout wooden stick with a flat base specially made for making porridge) is useful for making porridge but it is pretty much essential for making oatmeal: it is very difficult to make smooth oatmeal without one. A spurtle is useful even if you make your oatmeal in the microwave.

TOASTED OAT CEREAL WITH HONEY AND VANILLA

This is a scrumptious cross between granola and muesli which is surprisingly easy to make. Keep an eye on the oats while they are toasting, though, they must be pleasantly crisp, not rock hard! It's very difficult to stop yourself from scoffing handfuls of this as soon as it's cool.

Makes 6–8 servings	Lightly grease a large baking tray and preheat the oven to 150ºC (fan oven) or equivalent.

Warm **4 tablespoons runny honey**, either on the hob, or for 10–20 seconds on High in the microwave to make it more free-flowing. Stir in **2 tablespoons rapeseed or sunflower oil** and ½ **teaspoon vanilla essence** (or to taste).

Put **225g (8oz) porridge oats** in a large bowl and stir in the honey mixture using two metal spoons until all the oats are coated. Spread over the prepared tray and bake for approximately 15 minutes, until the oats are pale golden and toasted (but not at all dark). Turn and stir the oats halfway through the cooking time with a fish slice.

Turn into a large heatproof bowl and stir in **110g–175g (4–6oz) sultanas and/or raisins** and **about a tablespoon golden linseeds** (if available). Stir everything together while the oats are still hot and leave to cool.

Serve with cold milk and fresh fruit. It will keep in an airtight container for a week or two.

You can add a few other bits and pieces to this basic mixture if you like: chopped dried apricots, for example, but it is gorgeous just as it is.

On an everyday basis, you might like to add a selection of seeds such as sunflower, pumpkin, linseed and hemp to a good-quality ready-made muesli, with some dried cranberries. Serve with cold milk or yoghurt and fresh or stewed fruit.

STEWED FRUIT: see Puddings page 112.

FRUIT COMPOTE WITH GREEK YOGHURT

This is a lovely old-fashioned dried fruit compote that you can serve warm or cold with Greek yoghurt (or natural yoghurt, if you prefer). You may like to spice it up a little bit with a touch of cinnamon, particularly during the winter.

Put the dried fruit into a saucepan and pour the boiling water over it. (You may also like to add a cinnamon stick to the fruit.) Cover and leave to soak for 30–40 minutes. Next bring to the boil, then turn the heat down and simmer, partially covered, for 30–40 minutes or until plump. Remove the cinnamon stick and serve the compote warm or cold.

Be sure to warn everyone about the stones in the prunes and the possibility of the odd stray one in the peaches and apricots.

SERVES 4

500g (approx. 1lb) bag of
   dried fruit selection
   (sometimes called dried
   fruit salad) which
   includes: prunes, peaches,
   apricots, apples and pears
570ml (1 pint) boiling water

STRAWBERRY SMOOTHIE

If you are lucky enough to have a glut of strawberries in your garden or you have gone a bit mad at the Pick Your Own farm this smoothie recipe will put them to good use. Drink for breakfast or any time at all.

Cut the strawberries into halves or quarters and put into either a blender or a juicer with the yoghurt and apple juice. Whiz together and taste. The strawberries may be perfectly ripe and sweet or you may need a little honey. Whiz again and push through a nylon sieve to remove all those pesky little seeds.

Alternatively, whiz the strawberries with the apple juice and 4 tablespoons of strawberry yoghurt. Strain, as before.

SERVES 1–2 but it's easy to
   make more

About 12 strawberries
4 tablespoons natural
   yoghurt
100ml (4fl oz) apple juice
Honey to taste

Buns and Rolls are always welcome for a relaxed breakfast and nice to offer if you have people staying. See the **Making Your Own Bread** section: **Breakfast Buns** are particularly good and 'breakfasty'.

Orange and Almond Cake

Orange and Almond Cake served with a dollop of Greek or natural yoghurt makes a gorgeous breakfast. If you have some strawberries to slice alongside as well, that would be breakfast heaven.

See the **Cakes** section page 158 for recipe.

Marmalade Squares

Marmalade Squares are also good served at breakfast time: if they are a couple of days old, spread with a little butter.

See the **Cakes** section page 163 for recipe.

Grapefruit

Half a grapefruit is a refreshing way to start breakfast: a specially curved double-edged grapefruit knife is useful to cut through the segments: in fact it's difficult to separate the segments without one. Pink grapefruit is a little sweeter than regular grapefruit: try serving either with a sweet fruit such as strawberries or dried cranberries.

Freshly Squeezed Orange Juice

Nothing in a bottle or carton can completely capture the taste of freshly squeezed oranges so it is worth making a jug for special occasions. Incidentally, if you are making a recipe that calls for orange zest, juice the rest of the orange immediately and drink it so as not to waste it: otherwise it will shrivel and dry up, alone and forlorn at the back of the fridge.

LIGHT LUNCHES AND MIDWEEK SUPPERS

There's a good selection of lighter meals in this section
plus a few ideas that are more 'serving suggestions' than actual recipes.

GREEN SOUP (LABOUR OF LOVE SOUP)

You might want to call this Green Soup because the main ingredient is peas. Alternatively, it could be called Labour of Love Soup as it is a bit of a fiddle pushing the peas through a sieve or rotary food mill. If you don't do this the pea skins give the finished soup a rough texture which isn't as nice. Also you do need to process all the ingredients, not just the peas. Processing seems to release much more flavour and gives a smoother texture as well as distributing the oil from the onions throughout. It is worth it though: topped off with bacon and croutons it is a really delicious and nourishing winter meal.

SERVES 4

450g (1lb) frozen peas

Approximately 450g (1lb) potatoes, floury type if possible

2 or 3 carrots

1 parsnip, if available

2 or 3 sticks of celery, preferably including leaves

1 large onion

1 or 2 leeks, if available

Oil for frying

A little sea salt and freshly ground white pepper

To serve: fried diced bacon, croutons, freshly ground black pepper

Cook the peas in the normal way for 8–10 minutes. Peel and prepare the potatoes as you would normally for mash. Peel the carrots and parsnip, clean the celery. Add the carrots, parsnip and celery to the potatoes and cook all together for 20–25 minutes or until tender.

Put the peas in the food processor with a little of their cooking water and whiz to a purée. Push through a sieve or a rotary food mill and set aside.

Peel and dice the onion and peel, clean and slice the leek. Cook gently in the oil until soft but not coloured. You can put a lid on the pan if you like.

Strain the cooked potatoes and other vegetables and reserve the cooking water. Remove the bits of celery and discard. Mash the potatoes, parsnip and carrots together and put into the food processor with the onion and leek. Whiz together until smooth. Put into a large clean pan with the peas and stir together. Stir in some of the cooking water until you have the thickness you like. Season to taste with salt and a few twists of white pepper, and heat through.

To serve: fry some diced bacon in a little oil and in another pan fry a couple of slices of bread cut into small squares in a little oil. Serve the soup in deep bowls with the bacon and croutons and some freshly ground black pepper.

Garlic Croutons and Marmite Croutons
For garlic croutons spread the bread very lightly with garlic butter.
For Marmite croutons spread the lightest smear of Marmite over both sides of the bread before you slice it and fry it.

LEEK AND POTATO SOUP WITH ALL-IN-ONE STOCK

This is a real favourite. Leeks give soup a lovely silky consistency and are always worth adding to any vegetable soup. It's no trouble to add a few traditional stock vegetables to the cooking water and make a natural tasting integral stock. As with mashed potatoes, hot milk gives a better consistency than cold, which turns them a bit gluey and gloopy, so warm your milk before adding to the soup.

Peel and slice the onions. Peel and slice the leeks, discarding the tough green parts. Fry the leeks and onions gently in the butter until soft and translucent but not coloured. You can put a lid on the pan if you like, so they half fry, half steam.

Peel the potatoes and cut into chunks. Peel the carrots and cut lengthways and then in half. Don't cut them any smaller: you want some exposed surfaces so that maximum flavour can come out but you don't want too many bits to fish out later. Clean and trim the celery and cut in the same way. Add the carrot and celery to the potatoes and boil in unsalted water until tender.

Drain the potatoes, reserving the cooking water, and remove and discard the carrot and celery.

Roughly mash the potatoes with a fork and put them into the bowl of your food processor with the softened onions and leeks. Add about five tablespoons of the cooking water, some pepper and salt and whiz. Scrape the mixture down from the sides and add another four or five tablespoons of cooking water. Repeat and then add the warm milk. Check for seasoning, you may need more salt, and put into a clean pan and warm through. Add more cooking water for a thinner consistency.

Serve with crusty bread; a few chives snipped over the top look very professional.

Approximately 4 servings

1 large onion
350g (¾lb) leeks
25g (1oz) butter
700g (1½lb) potatoes
2 carrots
3–4 sticks of celery
Freshly ground white
   pepper
Salt to taste
100ml (4fl oz) semi-
   skimmed milk, warmed

THICK PEA AND HAM SOUP

This is a really old-fashioned pea soup, the kind made with dried peas that you soak overnight. You can get your ham knuckle from your local butcher at a very reasonable price. The soup won't be bright green like a soup made with fresh peas but a kind of murky yellow as in the London 'pea-souper' fogs of Victorian times.

SERVES 4–6

1 ham knuckle
450g (1lb) dried split peas
1 large onion
Oil for frying
1–2 carrots, peeled and
   cut into strips
2–3 sticks celery, trimmed
   and cut into strips
1 bay leaf
Freshly ground white or
   black pepper, if liked

You may need to soak your ham knuckle overnight if it's very salty; check with your butcher.

Soak the peas in cold water overnight. When you are ready to make the soup, drain them and try to get them as dry as possible. Try using two colanders: drain them in one, put a clean tea towel in the other, transfer them and fold the cloth over. If you put the peas into the hot oil when they are wet, they will spit all over your hands and wrists in a very painful way!

Peel and slice the onion and fry in the oil until soft and just starting to colour. Put the peas into the pan and turn and coat with the oil. Put the ham into a large saucepan and add the onions and peas, carrot, celery and bay leaf. Pour enough water over to cover; this will probably be about 3 litres (6 pints) or so. Bring to the boil, skim off any froth and simmer fairly briskly for two to three hours, stirring from time to time, or until the peas are soft and the ham is falling off the bone. Add more water if necessary.

Take the ham and the bay leaf out, drain off some of the liquid and reserve. Whiz all the rest in a food processor or blender in two batches. Have a clean pan standing by. If the soup seems a bit thick add some of the reserved cooking liquid. Using a dinner fork, take all the ham off the bone. You can add some of the ham to the soup if you like or use it for sandwiches to serve with the soup. Check for seasoning. You are unlikely to need salt and you may not need pepper either as the flavour is so lovely as it is. Make sure the soup is completely warmed through: it will spit and gloop like a primeval swamp so a spatter guard is useful.

Serve with plenty of crusty bread or sandwiches made from the ham and a touch of mustard. The ham makes gorgeous sandwiches: it's not unlike a hammy version of salt beef.

LENTIL SOUP WITH A TOUCH OF CURRY

This is another 'winter warmer' type soup, but somehow the curry flavour makes it equally welcome on a wet and chilly summer's day.

Wash the lentils in cold water and drain. Try to get them as dry as possible. The only downside of this soup is that lentils are such messy, clingy little creatures and you can end up with them stuck to practically everything!

Peel and slice the onion and fry in the oil until soft and just beginning to colour. A wide wok-style pan is perfect for this. Stir in the curry paste. Add the carrots and celery and the drained lentils and turn and stir them in the hot oil until they are all coated (the carrots and celery don't need to be softened, just coated). Finally, add the water and bay leaf.

Bring to the boil then turn down and simmer fairly briskly for about an hour or until the lentils are soft and most of the water has been absorbed. Stir from time to time and add more water if necessary. The soup will spit so cover the pan with a spatter guard or rest the lid loosely across the top.

Once it has cooked, remove the bay leaf and whiz the soup in a processor or blender until smooth. Check for seasoning. If you are not serving it immediately, transfer to a clean pan and keep warm on a low heat. This is really good served with warm naan bread or chapatti. If you have the time and energy, a garnish of onions, fried until they are quite dry and crispy, works well.

SERVES 4

225g (8oz) red split lentils
I large onion
Oil for frying
I level dessertspoonful of curry paste, such as Madras
2–3 carrots, peeled and cut fairly small
2–3 sticks of celery, trimmed and cut fairly small
I bay leaf
845ml (1½ pints) water

Sweetcorn Chowder with Bacon and Cod

You need creamed sweetcorn for this but it's not always easy to get hold of. You also need firm, waxy potatoes as floury ones will break up too easily.

SERVES 2

225g (½lb) potatoes
1 medium onion
1 red chilli pepper (or half
   if you prefer)
418g tin creamed
   sweetcorn
198g tin sweetcorn
   kernels, drained, or
   about 110g (4oz) frozen
   sweetcorn
Around 225g (½lb) of cod
   (or other firm white
   fish)
3–4 rashers of bacon
Freshly ground black
   pepper
Oil for frying

Peel the potatoes and cut into pieces slightly smaller than a postage stamp. Cook in boiling water until just tender; this should take five or ten minutes although potatoes can vary.

Slice the onion into small pieces and slice the chilli. Fry together gently until the onion is pale golden. Add the creamed sweetcorn and sweetcorn kernels. Add the potatoes together with their cooking water, and simmer everything together for ten minutes or so. Cut the fish into cubes a fraction bigger than the potato and add to the chowder. Meanwhile, cut the bacon into dice and fry until almost crisp. The chowder is ready when the fish is cooked through. Check for seasoning; you may need a touch of salt. Serve in deep bowls with the bacon on top and plenty of crusty bread and butter.

HOME-MADE VEGETABLE STOCK

Vegetable stock is simple and rewarding to make. Use it for soups, casseroles and gravy. The quantities below are approximate

Wash and cut the celery into several pieces. Peel the carrots and cut lengthways and then in half again: you want exposed surfaces so that maximum flavour and goodness can come out into the stock.

Remove the outer skin from the onion, and slice into several pieces. Put the sliced onion into a pan with the carrot, celery, celery leaves, bay leaf and a few peppercorns and pour in the water. Bring to the boil and simmer, uncovered, until the vegetables are soft. Cool and strain. If you are not using the stock immediately, cover and store in the fridge for up to 24 hours.

If you would like to give your stock a golden colour and the inner papery skin of the onion (the thin papery skin immediately next to the onion flesh) is clean and undamaged, add it to the stock: it will colour it beautifully.

1–2 sticks celery, plus
   leaves if possible
1–2 carrots
1 onion
1 bay leaf
Black or white
   peppercorns (optional)
425ml–1 litre (¾ –1¾ pints)
   water

Washing salad leaves

When washing salad leaves lower them *gently* into a bowl of cold water; don't wash them under running water or agitate them violently or they will bruise and tear. Lift them out gently onto a clean dry tea towel and fold it over them lightly to absorb most of the water then transfer to a second dry tea towel to dry completely. Any leftover leaves can be wrapped in a damp tea towel and stored in the fridge until the following day.

GREEN SALAD

Just a few crisp fresh lettuce leaves served with a little home-made salad dressing are always a welcome and refreshing part of any meal. You can add some peeled and thinly sliced cucumber and some thinly sliced celery as well if you like and maybe a scattering of peppery cress (watercress, or mustard cress). If you grow your own courgettes they are good raw (no need to peel), either grated or very thinly sliced in ribbons with a swivel peeler. If you grow both green and gold, they look attractive served together.

BABY LEAF SALAD

A selection of mixed baby leaves with a light drizzle of dressing is another welcome treat: thinly sliced celery and a little pile of grated carrot or matchsticks of young raw beetroot complement them beautifully.

BABY LEAF SALAD WITH BACON AND EGGS AND CROUTONS

This is great for lunch or as a starter if you are entertaining.

Selection of baby leaves such as: rocket, mizuna, spinach, mustard, pak choi, claytonia

Bacon, cut into small strips or squares

1 egg per person

Slices of decent bread, preferably not completely fresh

Oil for frying

Simple Home-Made Salad Dressing (see page 26)

Wash and dry the salad leaves (handle them gently) and arrange in the serving bowl or bowls. Fry the bacon until fairly crisp and hard-boil the eggs for 7–8 minutes *only* and plunge into cold water. Peel and cut into halves or quarters. Cut the bread into postage stamp size squares and fry in hot oil, lower the heat to moderate once they are in the pan and keep an eye on them, turning from time to time, until they are crisp and golden.

Just before serving, pile the bacon and croutons on top of the salad leaves, arrange the eggs on top and hand round the dressing in a jug.

GROW YOUR OWN BABY LEAF SALAD

Baby leaf salads are delicious but they can be expensive to buy. As they are so small they don't stay fresh for very long and it's much nicer (and more nutritious) to grow your own. In many ways it's much easier to grow them in containers than in the ground as it makes monitoring their growth and harvesting simpler. If you have an unheated greenhouse, cold frame or handy porch you can grow them most of the year round: in fact they grow better during the cooler months than during the height of summer when they can dry out too easily and become stressed.

The kind of plastic troughs you sometimes see spring bulbs growing in are ideal for baby leaf salad and they are quite inexpensive to buy. Alternatively, you can improvise with other containers: make a few drainage holes in a slightly battered old plastic storage box, for example. Armed with some packets of seed, good-quality potting compost, a pair of scissors for harvesting and a watering can you are all set.

Put a few crocks in the bottom of the trough(s) and fill with compost. Firm the top and water thoroughly. Sieve a little compost carefully over the surface (so the seeds can nestle comfortably) and sow the seeds fairly thinly over the top. Sieve a little more compost over them and label: it's useful to include the sowing date on the label. Keep an eye on them and once they start to come through, water gently with a fine rose as the compost starts to dry out.

Once the leaves start to take on recognisable shape you can start to harvest them with scissors. At this stage, remove the rose from your watering can and only water the roots. You will probably be able to take three cuts from them in all. If you really want to pamper them, give them a weak feed of something like seaweed extract after the first cut. When you want to sow some fresh seed, scrape the top compost off, add some fresh and sow fresh seed and after a few months tip it all out and start again with completely fresh compost. (The old compost can be used to mulch your flower beds.)

Suggestions for sowing

Here are some suggestions; try three or four kinds to start with and you will soon find the ones you like best. It's nice to have maybe half a dozen on the go at any one time. Chervil and dill are included as, though strictly speaking herbs, they are nice to add to a salad. When you eat baby leaves moments after harvesting you can really taste the goodness and vitality bursting out of them!

Baby spinach • Buckler leaf sorrel • Chervil • Claytonia (miner's lettuce or winter purslane) • Corn salad (lamb's lettuce or mache) • Dill: best grown in a deep pot • Fenugreek • Land cress • Mustard (red and gold varieties) • Mizuna • Pak choi • Rocket • Saltwort • Tatsoi

Some of these grow particularly well during the winter including: mizuna, rocket, tatsoi, claytonia and pak choi. Corn salad is very prone to mildew through the winter and claytonia is reluctant to grow after April. Buckler leaf sorrel is very happy in the ground but it is very invasive after a while and it's difficult to catch the leaves at their tenderest.

SIMPLE HOME-MADE SALAD DRESSING

It's very easy to make your own salad dressing: all you need is a screw-top jar. If you have one with a plastic lid, like the ones peanut butter comes in, so much the better as vinegar reacts with metal.

I heaped teaspoon Dijon
mustard

I level teaspoon runny
honey

3 tablespoons oil (mild
olive, rapeseed or
sunflower)

I tablespoon cider vinegar

Spoon the mustard and honey into the screw-top jar, add the oil and vinegar, screw the top on firmly and shake vigorously.

Variations
You can use wine vinegar if you prefer, make a special dressing with sherry vinegar or balsamic vinegar, add a little garlic, freshly ground black or white pepper, a touch of sea salt or use wholegrain mustard. Keep to the basic proportions of 3 parts oil and 1 part vinegar. Stick to tablespoons if you can as this works well in relation to the teaspoon measurement for honey and mustard.

Classic Potato Salad with Mayonnaise

*Potato salad is mainly thought of as a cold dish but it is also very good hot, especially with sausages (or try with **Proper Home-Made Hamburgers** (see page 41 for recipe), a green salad, mustard and gherkins).*

Peel the potatoes if you wish, or scrub gently and leave the skin on. Cut into bite-size pieces and boil or steam until just tender.

Drain and stir in the mayonnaise gently; a small wooden spoon is ideal, you don't want the potatoes to break up. Finish with a good grinding of black pepper and some snipped chives just before serving.

Potato Salad extras
Bacon fried until fairly crisp, cut into matchsticks or squares and scattered over. Potato salad with bacon and hard-boiled eggs is a meal in itself with a little green salad on the side.

Similarly, sliced freshly cooked sausages mixed into the potato salad while it is still hot makes a great quick meal: try mixing some mustard into the mayonnaise and slicing some gherkins over the top; hard-boiled eggs would also be a nice addition.

Just a *few* snipped anchovies and plenty of freshly ground black pepper.

Potatoes, preferably waxy
Mayonnaise to coat
Freshly ground black
    pepper
Small amount of very
    finely chopped onion or
    snipped chives, or both

CLASSIC COLESLAW WITH MAYONNAISE

1 small white cabbage
1 carrot
¼ a white onion, possibly
   less, sliced very finely
Mayonnaise to coat
Splash of cider vinegar
   (about a teaspoon)
Freshly ground black
   pepper

Some people may like their coleslaw 'chunky style' but generally it's best to slice the cabbage as finely as possible.

Cut the cabbage in half and remove the inner core. Lay each half flat on a board and slice as finely as you can or put through the slicing attachment of a food processor. If you are slicing by hand cut across the slices as well to avoid people having to cope with long strings of mayonnaisy cabbage dangling from their mouths as they eat!
Peel or scrub and grate the carrot. Cut the onion into the very finest pieces you can; too much raw onion taste can be overpowering. Mix everything together thoroughly with enough mayonnaise to coat and the cider vinegar. Finish with a good grinding of black pepper.

Variations
The heart of a very fresh green cabbage works just as well as white cabbage.

Grated celeriac or parsnip combines well with the other ingredients.

Some diced cheese scattered over the top is a nice addition: mild cheeses cut into dice without crumbling more easily than mature cheeses.

CELERY, APPLE AND WALNUT SALAD

This is a great combination of textures and flavours.

Slice the celery and apple (no need to peel) and mix with the rest of the ingredients.

This is lovely served with some green salad and cold chicken or ham.

Quantities to suit of:
Celery
Crisp eating apple
Shelled walnuts, halves,
   broken or pieces
Raisins
Mayonnaise to coat
Freshly ground black
   pepper

New Potatoes and Green Olives

New potatoes and **green olives** are a happy combination. If you like **anchovies**, just a few snipped over the top go beautifully too.

Kidney Beans and Sweetcorn with Chives

A tin of **kidney beans**, drained and refreshed in cold water, mixed with a similar quantity of **sweetcorn**, is another good combination with a few **chives** snipped over the top. This is a great quick summer lunch with some tuna and a few salad leaves and some cold potatoes.

Watermelon and Feta Cheese

This is a lovely refreshing salad for summer: the feta and watermelon go beautifully together. Put a little extra honey in the salad dressing as it goes so well with the salty, fresh-tasting feta. You can serve it on its own as a first course or with a green salad as a light meal. You may prefer it without the olives.

Quantities to suit of: Watermelon, cubed Feta cheese, cubed, about the same amount as of watermelon Salad dressing (see recipe on page 26) Freshly ground black pepper Black olives, if liked	Mix the watermelon and feta cheese together gently, either in individual serving bowls or one big one. Drizzle the salad dressing over with a little grinding of black pepper. Top with a few black olives and, if you have any mint handy, a few leaves scattered over everything looks appetising. Serve immediately.

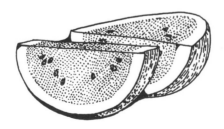

GREEK-STYLE SALAD

This is great on its own or as an accompaniment to Moussaka.

As with the previous salad, put a little extra honey in the dressing as the feta and honey combine so beautifully together. Greek salads are fairly chunky and hearty so cut the tomatoes into quarters and the cucumber into chunks. Cube the feta. Arrange the lettuce leaves in the bottom of your serving dish or dishes and pile the tomatoes, cucumber, olives and feta over the top. Pour the salad dressing over just before serving and scatter the oregano or basil leaves over.

You may also like to add some thinly sliced red onion and chunks of red and yellow pepper.

Quantities to suit of:
Cos lettuce
Tomatoes
Cucumber
Feta cheese
Black olives
Salad dressing (see recipe on page 26)
Fresh oregano or basil leaves to finish, if available

LIGHTLY CURRIED CHICKEN SALAD

This is very like Coronation Chicken but much lighter and less rich.

Mix together about a level teaspoon each of apricot conserve and curry paste to a couple of tablespoons of mayonnaise and a small handful of sultanas. Mix together with the chicken. This quantity will serve two adults so adjust quantities where necessary. You can now serve this with a salad, with rice, as a sandwich filling or with a baked potato.

Quantities to suit of:
Cold chicken, shredded
Apricot conserve
Madras curry paste
Mayonnaise
Sultanas

An omelette is such a simple and delicious meal: the eggs should be as fresh as possible. It's best to use a smallish pan for omelettes as they need to be quite thick: if your pan is too large you will end up with a flat, eggy pancake rather than a tempting plump omelette. The pan also needs to have a fairly thick bottom to prevent the omelette from getting too hot and sticking and burning.

PLAIN OMELETTE

Use **3 eggs** per person with **a little sea salt** to season, possibly **a little black pepper** and **a little oil** or **butter** to grease the pan.

Beat the eggs gently in a bowl: don't over-beat.

Grease the bottom of the pan lightly – you don't need a layer of oil or anything – and put the pan on to heat. Once the pan is hot, tip in the eggs and turn the heat down to moderate. After a moment or two, lift up the edges with a fish slice or spatula as the egg starts to set, and tip the pan from side to side so that the unset egg runs underneath and makes contact with the pan. Continue until the egg has all set and the top is just cooked. Flip one side of the omelette onto the other so it is folded in half. Slide onto the serving plate. The pan should now be dry and not oily at all.

Serve with a green salad.

CHEESE OMELETTE

Make the omelette as above and once the top is almost set, scatter about **25g (1oz) grated cheese** over the surface. Fold the omelette as before and the cheese will melt in the heat of the omelette.

HERB OMELETTE (OMELETTE AUX FINES HERBES)

Again make the omelette as before, and just before the top is completely set add a scattering of **finely chopped soft (not woody) herbs** such as the traditional **parsley, chives, chervil** and **French tarragon**. Fold and serve as before.

MACARONI CHEESE

Here are two variations of a well-known and much-loved dish. You will notice that the sauce is made with cornflour rather than a butter and flour roux. It can be much easier to blend cornflour and milk together for a sauce than it is to make it with a roux of butter and plain wheat flour and then add milk. Also, particularly when adding cheese, you may prefer not to have the extra butter, and best of all: the resulting sauce is very smooth!

CLASSIC MACARONI CHEESE

You don't always have to use actual macaroni: try penne or rigatoni or, best of all, cavatappi, which has an appealing wiggly shape. Serve with a green salad or a cooked green vegetable and possibly some garlic bread. Tomato ketchup is always welcome.

Cook the pasta in the usual way: don't overcook. Using a heavy-bottomed milk saucepan, mix the cornflour and dry mustard together and then add a little of the milk and mix to a smooth paste. Gradually add the rest of the milk, stirring as you add. Turn on the heat and bring to boiling point, stirring all the time. Turn down and simmer for a minute or two, stirring constantly. Remove from the heat and stir in most of the grated cheese. Season with pepper and pour over the drained, cooked pasta. Sprinkle the top with the rest of the cheese and bake in a moderate oven until lightly golden and bubbling on top.

✓ **Useful Note:** Although Cheddar is best for the actual sauce, you can experiment with grating different types of cheese over the top: try smoked Cheddar, for example.

SERVES 2–3

225g (8oz) macaroni or other tube-style pasta
2 heaped tablespoons cornflour
Generous pinch of dry mustard
570ml (1 pint) semi-skimmed milk
225g (8oz) mature Cheddar, grated
Freshly ground black or white pepper

Red Hot Chilli and Mustard Macaroni Cheese

This is the same as above but with chilli peppers and extra mustard: cheese and chilli seem to go really well together. Snip some hot red chilli peppers with kitchen scissors (quantity according to your personal taste, but possibly a quarter to half of one for the nervous, or one or two of those tiny little hot chillies you can grow at home) into about a tablespoon of oil and fry gently until soft. Make the cheese sauce as above, but step up the mustard content a little. Stir the cooked chilli, with the oil, into the prepared cheese sauce and continue as above.

✓ **Useful Note:** If you would like to make a bit more of your topping, butter a slice or two of bread (mix a little garlic into the butter, if you like), cut into small squares and scatter over the top before you put the dish into the oven. Instant, integral, croutons!

Two-Way Tuna Pasta Sauce

This makes a great quick supper using ingredients from the kitchen cupboard. There are two versions here: Robust and Mild and Creamy. The second one is just the same as the first but has two or three teaspoons of cream added. The difference the cream makes is very marked: it's almost like a different dish! If you would prefer to use less oil, tuna in spring water is fine, but don't use tuna in brine: the anchovies are already very salty.

Serve with plenty of pasta shapes and steamed green beans.

Robust Tuna Pasta Sauce

SERVES 2–4

50g tin anchovies in oil
185g tin tuna in oil
4–5 tablespoons **Easy Tomato Sauce for Pasta** (see page 71) (or from a jar)
Freshly ground black pepper
2 teaspoons pickled capers

Snip the anchovies into a pan with their oil. Add the tuna with about half of the oil. Heat them together, stirring constantly to break up the anchovies and tuna, and stir in the tomato sauce and black pepper. Drain and rinse the capers and add to the pan. Heat until gently bubbling.

MILD AND CREAMY TUNA PASTA SAUCE

This is exactly the same as above, but just before serving, add **2–3 generous teaspoons of double cream** and heat through.

QUICK SPAGHETTI SUPPER

*This is a quick version of the well-known 'Pasta Puttenesca'. You can either use some **Easy Tomato Sauce for Pasta** (see page 71) if you have any made, or one from a jar.*

Snip the anchovies into pieces and fry gently in their own oil. Slice the chilli and add to the pan. It doesn't matter at all if the anchovy breaks up during cooking. Once the chilli has softened, stir in the tomato sauce and wine, if using. Chop the olives fairly finely, reserving a few to garnish, and add to the pan. If you feel up to chopping the capers, do so, otherwise add them whole. Simmer everything for half an hour or more until it has reduced slightly and has a 'jammier' consistency. Test for seasoning before serving; you may like a pinch of sugar.

Serve with pasta. You don't need a huge amount per serving: it's more of a generous *flavouring* for the pasta than anything else.

SERVES 2–4 but easy to
  increase quantity

50g tin anchovies
I red chilli (or half,
  depending on taste, or a
  pinch of chilli powder)
Roughly 400g (14oz)
  tomato pasta sauce
Slosh of red wine
  (optional)
Handful of pitted black
  olives
Teaspoon pickled capers,
  drained

TAGLIATELLE WITH POACHED EGGS

This is another really quick meal: more of a serving suggestion than a recipe. You need to work quickly though, as the eggs must be served immediately.

SERVES 2

Cook **225g (8oz) tagliatelle** in the usual way. Melt **150g (5oz) soft cheese** gently in a saucepan and poach **2 eggs** so that the whites are firm but the yolks are still runny.

Pile the tagliatelle onto each plate, top with the melted soft cheese and an egg. Season generously with **black pepper**. Cut into the eggs immediately so that the yolk combines with the soft cheese and pasta.

You may prefer a couple of eggs each and you may also like to buy soft cheese with black pepper already in it, or one with garlic.

QUICK PASTA WITH CHILLI AND MOZZARELLA

Again, this is really just a serving suggestion. This works with most kinds of pasta but rigatoni or penne work particularly well.

SERVES 2–4

Fry a **red chilli** in **a little oil** and add about **400g (14oz)** or so of **Easy Tomato Sauce for Pasta** (see page 71) or one from a jar. Add a splosh of **red wine** and **half a teaspoon of sugar**. Simmer gently for half an hour or so. Slice some **Mozzarella** thinly and serve the sauce over pasta with the thinly sliced Mozzarella melting over the top.

Quick Special Pasta with Smoked Salmon and Mascarpone

It's hard to believe that a dish that seems so special and luxurious should take so little time and effort to make!

Cook the pasta according to your usual method and drain. Heat the mascarpone gently in a saucepan until it becomes a smooth sauce. Cut the salmon into strips and stir briefly into the mascarpone (don't over-stir or overheat the salmon or it will start to break up). Remove from the heat. Season with black pepper and serve on top of the pasta with wedges of lemon. Perfect with a green salad (and preferably a glass of chilled white wine or champagne).

225g (8oz) pasta
(tagliatelle looks special
but shells are also good)
250g (9oz) tub of
mascarpone
Approximately 100g (4oz)
smoked salmon or a
little more
Freshly ground black
pepper and wedges of
lemon to serve

PASTA CARBONARA

Try to think of the carbonara part as a liberal coating for the pasta rather than a free-flowing sauce. Once you know you are simply coating the pasta with the combined egg and cream and not trying to make a perfect savoury custard type sauce (without curdling) in about five seconds flat before serving, it really helps. Egg yolks, rather than whole eggs, give a smoother texture. Serve with a green salad.

Use your own judgement in deciding how much pasta to allow per person. For every **225g (8oz)** pasta you need no more than **2 egg yolks** and **3 tablespoons of double cream**. You can use spaghetti, tagliatelle, linguine, or pasta shapes if you prefer.

Cook your pasta. Beat the egg yolks and cream lightly together.

Once the pasta is cooked, turn off the heat, drain the pasta quickly and return it to the dry pan. Pour the eggs and cream on top, stir briefly with a wooden spoon and put the lid back on for a few moments. Stir again briefly and serve immediately.

You may like to season with plenty of black pepper and maybe a touch of salt. You can top with finely grated (or shavings of) Parmesan or similar. Cheddar cheese, finely grated on a microplane, is also good. Matchsticks or little squares of fried bacon or garlic croutons go beautifully too, as do a few snipped anchovy fillets fried in their own oil.

Separating the eggs
Since you will be cooking the egg yolks only briefly, it is better not to separate the eggs just by tipping the yolk from one half of the shell to the other. You can use an egg separator or two dessertspoons work well. Alternatively, you can try **the egg cup trick**: this involves cracking the egg onto a small plate or saucer, holding an egg cup upside down over the yolk, and pouring off the white.

EGG FRIED RICE

This is a really adaptable recipe: you can add extra bits and pieces to suit yourself and what's in your fridge and garden. Add a little more oil to the pan than usual so you can coat the rice when you add it. You need a wide, ideally wok-style, pan for this.

Boil the rice in the normal way, add the peas for the last 3 minutes of cooking time (you may need to increase the total cooking time by a minute or two to compensate for the lowered temperature when the peas go in).

Fry the onion and celery for a few moments in a wide pan and then add the chilli and garlic. Stir in the Chinese Five Spice Powder. Add the sweetcorn and stir to coat in the oil. Add the drained, cooked rice and peas and stir to coat in the oil. Stir the egg through the rice and continue cooking for a few moments.

Serve immediately with a little ketjap manis (delicious sweet, thick Indonesian soy type sauce) or soy sauce.

Extra bits and pieces
You can add anything else you fancy such as: florets of broccoli, sliced mushrooms, sliced red or yellow peppers, sliced courgettes, baby sweetcorn, and top with fried bacon, garlic or Marmite croutons, cashew nuts, or a handful of fresh peas from the garden.

Cooking the egg differently
You may prefer the egg slightly set before you stir it into the rice. If so, either cook it in a separate pan for a few moments until it is just starting to set and then ease it into the rice and stir gently, or if you have enough room in the rice pan, clear a space at the bottom of the pan and cook the egg for a few moments before stirring it through.

Rice with fried egg on top
Alternatively, fry an egg separately for each person and sit each one on top of the rice when you serve it.

SERVES 2–4

225g (8oz) rice, easy cook is fine

50g (2oz) frozen peas

1 small onion, sliced, or 1 bunch of spring onions including the more delicate green parts, sliced

1 celery stick, thinly sliced

1 red chilli (or to taste)

1 garlic clove, finely sliced, or a little minced garlic from a jar

½ teaspoon Chinese Five Spice Powder (or to taste)

50g (2oz) frozen sweetcorn

Oil for frying

2 eggs, lightly beaten

Hot Ways with Couscous

Couscous here refers to the instant kind where you just add hot water to the grains, which have already been partially cooked, and not the authentic North African kind that is steamed in a couscoussiere over cooking vegetables. The instant couscous that we have become used to is quick and easy, nourishing and extremely adaptable. A little plain couscous makes a good alternative to plain boiled rice to give to a child recovering from a stomach upset. Couscous is popular served cold as a salad but it's also good served hot.

Couscous can be cooked very plainly by simply adding hot water or stock but you can fry some onions in a little oil and then add the dry couscous to the pan, stirring to coat the couscous, as you would with a risotto, before adding the liquid.

Couscous with Bacon and Egg

This is a surprisingly comforting dish. Add a touch of garlic if you like when you add the chilli. If you can find any of that gorgeous thick, sweet, soy-based Indonesian 'ketjap manis' to drizzle over it all, that would be just perfect.

SERVES 2	Fry the onion in the oil until just starting to brown. Add the chilli and celery to the pan halfway through the cooking time. Add the sweetcorn and stir everything together.
I small onion, finely sliced	
Oil for frying	
½ red chilli, finely sliced	
I stick celery, very thinly sliced	Meanwhile, fry the bacon and eggs. Finally, add the couscous to the fried vegetables, stir thoroughly to coat, add the hot water, leave to stand for about five minutes and fluff with a fork.
Approximately 50g (2oz) frozen sweetcorn	
2–3 rashers back bacon, cut into small squares or strips	Pile a mound of couscous onto each plate and scatter the bacon over it and top with a fried egg.
2 eggs	
200g (7oz) couscous	
200ml (8fl oz) hot water	

Couscous with Chicken and Ham

This is the same as above but instead of bacon and eggs, serve topped with **shredded cold chicken** and **ham**.

PROPER HOME-MADE HAMBURGERS

Proper home-made hamburgers (called hamburgers because they originally caught on in Hamburg, not because they are made of ham) are really delicious and you know exactly what is in them, particularly if you buy your meat from a butcher's shop. Also they are really easy to make. They are a real treat with chunky chips or a baked potato, sesame buns, salad, mayonnaise, relishes, ketchup, mustard, gherkins and the whole works, but they are also good with mashed potatoes, plenty of gravy and hot vegetables.

If you are going to make these quite often, it's worth getting one of those inexpensive little plastic burger presses: they may look a bit gimmicky but they are quite robust and can last for years. You also need some waxed paper or cellophane discs. If you have difficulty getting hold of them your butcher may be able to help. If you don't have a burger press you can easily shape them by hand: it is easier to shape them with wet hands, rather than floured. Alternatively, you can get quite good results from pressing them into a round metal biscuit cutter: a small round glass jar, such as a mustard jar, is useful to press the meat down with. Keep the lid on as it makes it easier to handle.

Burgers from ready-minced beef are fine but they don't stay together very well. It's a much better idea to process your meat at home in a food processor with the bread and onion and seasoning. This way everything melds together and the resulting burger is firmer and much more delicious. Some keen home-made burger lovers may use best rump steak, but apart from the extravagance, the cheaper cuts – chuck, blade and skirt – all have a wonderful flavour and cook particularly well as burgers.

Tear the bread into small pieces and put into the bowl of your food processor with the onion. Cut the steak into smaller pieces, season with the salt and pepper and put into the processor. Whiz everything together, stopping the machine from time to time and stirring it round slightly. Once the mixture has started to cling together stop the machine and *remove the blade*. You can now take the meat mixture out with your hands without fear of cutting yourself! Shape into burgers (see above).

Fry them in a little oil (you can grill them, if you prefer); keep the heat moderate in both cases. Try using two fish slices to help you turn them over. Allow 10–20 minutes' cooking time.

These burgers are very plain but you can season them more specifically if you like. Try adding a good pinch of mustard powder and a few shakes of Worcestershire sauce to the mix, or some Tabasco, finely sliced chilli, or some herbs.

Frozen hamburgers
The burgers freeze really well: make sure you freeze them with discs of waxed paper or cellophane between them so you can separate them easily. You can cook them from frozen, just allow a few extra minutes' cooking time.

You can also go mad and make your own baps as well: see **Making Your Own Bread** section for recipe.

MAKES 4–6 burgers, but it's easy to double the quantity

50g (2 oz) bread, white or wholemeal
1 small onion, peeled and sliced
225g (8oz) chuck, blade, or skirt steak
½ teaspoon salt
Freshly ground black or white pepper
Oil for frying

SIMPLE FISH CAKES

Fish cakes are great for a quick lunch or supper, or even for a relaxed breakfast. This is a very flexible recipe that works with most types of fish. Once you get into the swing of it you can add more varied seasonings to suit whichever fish you are using. A good general rule is to use equal amounts of fish and potato: otherwise you will have a fish-flavoured potato cake!

225g (8oz) cod, haddock or similar white fish, skin and bones removed

225g (8oz) potato, mashed with a little butter and hot milk (prepared weight)

Freshly ground black or white pepper

Either approximately 50g (2oz) cornflakes or 110g (4oz) bread, preferably a little on the dry side

Approximately 1 tablespoon flour

1 egg, lightly beaten

Oil for frying

Fry the fish gently in a lightly oiled pan until it has lost its translucence and is opaque and fully cooked. Flake gently into the mashed potatoes. It is easier if the potatoes are still warm and are of a fairly firm consistency (although everything needs to be cool enough to handle). Season and stir gently to mix.

If you are using breadcrumbs, tear the bread into rough pieces and, using a food processor, whiz into fine crumbs. Tip into a dry frying pan (no oil) and heat on the hob over a moderate heat for a few minutes, stirring constantly with a wooden spoon or spatula. This is to dry out the crumbs and crisp them up a bit.

If you are using cornflakes, put them onto one half of a clean dry tea towel, fold the other half over, and roll vigorously with a rolling pin until you have fine crumbs. Alternatively, roll between two pieces of greaseproof paper.

Once the crumbs are ready, tip them into a shallow dish and heat some oil in a frying pan over a moderate heat.

Divide the fish cake mixture into four and shape into cakes with floured hands. Roll in flour and flatten slightly. If you would prefer them to have more of a formal shape, roll them along sideways to give them a distinct edge.

Dip each cake into the beaten egg, making sure it is fully coated, and then in the breadcrumbs or crushed cornflakes.

Heat some oil in a pan and fry for approximately 10 minutes over a moderate heat, turning from time to time, until the fish cakes are completely cooked and the coating is golden.

If you prefer, you can miss out the beaten egg and crumbs stage and fry them just coated in flour.

Using other fish
You can also use fresh salmon for gorgeous salmon fish cakes or smoked cod or haddock for fabulous smoked fish cakes. Both of these are good served with a little mayonnaise on the side.

Tinned tuna and tinned salmon also make good fish cakes. Drain, and mix with a similar amount of potato.

Suggested extra seasonings
Finely chopped parsley, chervil, dill or chives, with white or smoked fish, tinned or fresh salmon.

Sliced red chilli fried briefly in a little oil, with tuna or white fish.

A little grated cheese, with smoked or white fish.

Finely grated lemon zest, with salmon.

Cheesy Potato Cakes

These are very simple indeed: mix **50g (2oz) grated Cheddar cheese** into **225g (8oz) potatoes**, mashed to a fairly stiff consistency with **butter** and a little **hot milk**, season with **freshly ground black pepper** and proceed as for **Simple Fish Cakes**, above.

POTATO CROQUETTES AND CHEESY POTATO CROQUETTES

These are exactly the same as above but shape into smaller cakes or fat cylinders. You can make them with or without the cheese. You may like to season the plain version with **a touch of salt**.

CHEESY CHILLI POTATO CAKES

You might like to spice up the **Cheesy Potato Cakes**, above, with some thin slices of **red chilli**, gently fried in a little oil.

POTATO AND PARSNIP CAKES

These are made from **equal amounts of plain mashed potato** (no cheese) and **parsnips, peeled and boiled until tender and mashed**. Season with **a little salt and pepper** and proceed as above. These are great served with sausages or a roast.

HAM KNUCKLE

This is the same cut as the one used for Thick Pea and Ham Soup (it is also known as ham hock). It is so good and so reasonably priced it is worth cooking just for the ham. It really is like a kind of hammy salt beef and makes great sandwiches with granary-style bread, plenty of mustard and some gherkins. It's also good with a couple of fried eggs and some fried potatoes. Speaking of eggs, another lovely snack with this ham is to have it with a freshly baked bap or roll and a soft-boiled egg, peeled like a hard-boiled egg and just broken on top of the shredded ham, with just a tiny twist of black pepper. (Soft-boiled eggs without their shells are called 'oeufs mollets', to give them their fancy name.)

You may need to soak your ham knuckle overnight if it's very salty; check with your butcher.

Put the ham into a large saucepan with the onion, carrot, celery, bay leaf and peppercorns. Pour enough water over to cover; this will probably be about 3 litres (6 pints) or so. Bring to the boil, skim off any froth and simmer fairly briskly for two to three hours, or until the ham is virtually falling off the bone. Check from time to time, adding more water if necessary.

Once cooked, take the ham from the cooking water, cover with foil and leave to rest in a warm place for 20–30 minutes. Use a dinner fork to take all the ham off the bone.

If you are making soup within the next 24 hours strain the cooking water, cool quickly and refrigerate to use as stock.

SERVES 2–4

1 ham knuckle
1 large onion, sliced
1–2 carrots, peeled and cut into strips
2–3 sticks of celery, trimmed and cut into strips
1 bay leaf
A few black or white peppercorns

QUICK SAUSAGE AND CRUSTY BREAD LUNCH

A couple of sausages make a great quick lunch served with **crusty bread** and **mustard**, with maybe a bit of **salad** on the side. If you have friends round you can go to town a bit more and maybe have two or three kinds of local sausages and a selection of different mustards and **chutney** or **relish**.

CAULIFLOWER CHEESE

Cauliflower Cheese is really underrated. It's a shame as it makes a lovely lunch or supper with some crusty bread and a bit of green salad on the side. It's also great with sausages or bacon and baked potatoes for a more substantial meal. Try it, too, served as an accompaniment with gammon steaks or baked ham. Although cauliflower should definitely never be cooked to a nasty sulphurous mush, it needs to be quite soft for cauliflower cheese so it can become amalgamated properly with the cheese sauce.

The sauce is made simply with cornflour and milk, rather than a butter and flour roux.

SERVES 2–4	Preheat oven to 160ºC (fan oven) or equivalent.
1 medium cauliflower 2 heaped tablespoons of cornflour Generous pinch of dry mustard 570ml (1 pint) semi-skimmed milk 225g (8 oz) mature Cheddar, grated Freshly ground black or white pepper	Break the cauliflower into florets and steam or boil until just soft but not mushy. You sometimes see pictures of cauliflower cooked whole, but in practice it's difficult to get it to cook evenly this way and much more difficult to serve and eat. Once cooked, leave the cauliflower to drain and make the sauce. Using a heavy-bottomed milk saucepan, mix the cornflour and dry mustard together and then add a little of the milk and mix to a smooth paste. Gradually add the rest of the milk, stirring as you add. Turn on the heat and bring to boiling point, stirring all the time. Turn down and simmer for a minute or two, stirring constantly. Remove from the heat and stir in most of the grated cheese. Season with pepper and pour over the drained, cooked cauliflower. Sprinkle the top generously with the rest of the cheese and bake in a moderate oven until lightly golden and bubbling on top. It will really retain the heat when it first comes out of the oven so leave it to settle for a few moments before serving. The resulting dish should be just the firm side of soft, with a thick smooth sauce and a slight hint of chewy melted cheese topping: in fact generally a comforting sort of consistency which contrasts nicely with the faintly bracing taste of the cauliflower.

Leeks in Cheese Sauce

Leeks are great in cheese sauce. Peel and clean the leeks and cut into thick slices. Steam until just soft or soften in a little butter or oil. Drain on kitchen paper and cover with cheese sauce as above.

Jansenn's Temptation

This is one of those fantastic dishes that can be a main course for late breakfast, lunch or supper or an accompaniment to something else. It works well with floury or waxy potatoes, peeled or unpeeled. If it is to be a meal it is perfect with salad and crusty bread with a bit of cheese and fruit to follow. As a side dish it works brilliantly with plainly cooked lamb or steak and a green vegetable such as steamed broccoli.

Heat oven to around 160ºC.

Peel the potatoes if you would like a more delicate look to the finished dish, or leave the skins on if not. If you are using new potatoes, you might like to leave them on. Cut into smallish pieces either lengthways or in circles. Cook in boiling water until just tender and drain.

Slice the onion into smallish pieces and fry until golden in the oil from the anchovies. Cut each anchovy into about 6 pieces and add to the onions for the last few minutes of cooking. The anchovies may break up completely during cooking but don't worry: it's the flavour you are after.

Everything should be cooked through and soft and succulent before it goes into the oven. Bear in mind that it's going into the oven to finish off and for the flavours to amalgamate, not to cook through as such.

Butter an ovenproof dish and cover the bottom with a layer of potatoes, grind on plenty of black pepper and then spread the onions and anchovies over the top. Finish with the rest of the potatoes and another grinding of pepper. You can put some of the onion mixture on top if you like but be aware it can burn quite easily. Pour over the cream, dot with butter and put into the oven for around 20 minutes or until golden. Don't have your heat too high or the cream will split. You might think butter on top is overdoing it a bit but it's not quite the same without.

Serve warm rather than scalding hot. Once you have experienced a Jansenn's Temptation burn on the roof of your mouth you will know why!

For 2 people as a main course, or 3 or 4 as a side dish, take the following quantities; for more, increase proportionally.

700–900g (1½–2lb) potatoes
1 medium onion
Tin or jar of anchovies
Small amount of butter
Freshly ground black pepper
250–300ml carton of cream, preferably double

KEDGEREE

This is a really lovely dish for a late breakfast, lunch or supper. Serve with hard-boiled eggs, lemon wedges, mango chutney and maybe a few sultanas fried in butter (yes, they are really delicious). Alternatively, try serving with fried eggs and tomato ketchup: a home-made fish cake or two on the side would also go down well (see earlier recipe).

Serves 2–3 on its own or
   4 with fish cakes

225g (8oz) or so of
   smoked haddock or
   smoked cod: smoked
   loin of cod is especially
   good
Oil for frying: 1–2
   tablespoons
1 medium onion
1 level dessertspoon
   Madras curry paste, or
   to taste (or use curry
   powder to your own
   taste, if you prefer)
225g (8oz) long-grain rice,
   easy cook rice is fine
570ml (1 pint) water
About 110g (4oz) or so
   frozen sweetcorn
   kernels (or tinned)
1 bay leaf
About 110g (4oz) or so
   button mushrooms,
   thinly sliced (optional)
Lemon to finish (optional)

Skin the fish (this is much easier if the fish is frozen and you remember to do it while it is partially defrosted), and remove any bones. Put the oil into a wide wok type pan to heat. Cut the onion lengthways, and then across, into pieces of roughly a centimetre, and fry in the oil until golden.

Stir in the curry paste or curry powder and continue stirring it around for a few moments to develop the flavour. Add the rice, stirring it through until each grain is coated. Pour the water in gradually, stirring as you go. Add the sweetcorn, the fish, the bay leaf, and the mushrooms, if using. Bring to simmering point and continue to simmer until the rice is cooked and the liquid has almost all been absorbed.

Don't stir too vigorously or the fish will turn to mush. You shouldn't need any salt as the fish is quite salty, plus there is salt in the curry paste. If the fish is still in large pieces, gently flake into smaller pieces. You may like to finish with a squeeze of lemon.

For something a bit special gently stir in a spoonful or two of cream before serving. If you want this effect but haven't any cream, a knob of butter works well.

✔ Useful Note on hard-boiled eggs
Hard-boiled eggs can be a delicious treat or a slippery, over-boiled nightmare! Bring the water to a fast boil and add the eggs at that point, and then set the timer and boil for seven to eight minutes *only*. Remove from the heat *immediately* and plunge into cold water. Roll the eggs briskly on a flat surface and peel off the shell.

QUICK SPECIAL STEAK AND MUSHROOM SUPPER

*This is an ideal quick and sustaining Friday night supper for two tired and hungry people. The mushrooms are virtually identical to the **Creamed Mushrooms on Toast** recipe from the **Very Quick Light Meals on Toast** section.*

Heat some oil in a pan on a fairly high heat. Add the steak and cook briefly on both sides, then turn down the heat to moderate. Cook to your liking, turning a couple of times.

Meanwhile, heat some oil in another pan and cook the mushrooms over a moderate heat: put a lid on the pan so that the mushrooms half fry, half steam, until they are soft and succulent. Add the garlic towards the end of the cooking time. Once the mushrooms and garlic are cooked through, drain away any excess liquid, stir in the cream and turn up the heat so that the cream bubbles and reduces and slightly darkens in colour, stirring throughout. Season with black pepper and a touch of salt.

Once the steak has cooked, remove from the pan and keep warm. Splash a little sherry vinegar into the juices left in the steak pan and turn up the heat for a few moments, let the vinegar sizzle, and scrape off and stir in any sticky residue from the bottom. Turn off the heat, pour in the creamy mushroom mixture and stir together.

Serve the mushrooms on top of the steak. This is perfect served with new potatoes in season or some tagliatelle, and steamed broccoli, and possibly a heartening glass of red wine.

2 nice pieces of fillet steak
Oil for frying
250g (9oz) mushrooms, closed cap, button, chestnut or a mixture, sliced
1 finely chopped garlic clove, or a little minced garlic from a jar
6 tablespoons or so of double cream
Freshly ground black pepper and a little sea salt
Splash of sherry vinegar (2–3 teaspoons)

Main Meals

Here is a selection of hearty main meals,
including some familiar old favourites,
for family meals and informal entertaining.

Beef Stew and Dumplings

This is the sort of dish that makes you feel better about the weather getting colder. Dumplings seem to have fallen out of favour recently but they are so tasty and very easy to make. People seem to assume that dumplings are heavy and stodgy but freshly cooked dumplings are actually quite light in texture. The parsnips give the stew a lovely warm, sweet flavour. Serve the dumplings as soon as they are ready: they need to be eaten while they are fresh and hot.

SERVES 4

For the stew
450–500g (1lb) braising or preferably feather steak (ask your local butcher)
1–2 tablespoons plain flour
A little oil for frying
1 large onion, sliced
1 generous tablespoon black treacle
1 tablespoon Worcestershire sauce
1 tablespoon tomato purée
Approximately 1¼ litres (2 pints) hot water
1 bay leaf
2 or 3 carrots, peeled and cut slantwise, into wedges
2 or 3 small parsnips, peeled and cut slantwise, into wedges
Black or white pepper, freshly ground

To make the stew
Cut the meat into bite-sized cubes and coat in the flour. Fry the meat in hot oil in a wide pan until lightly browned. Once the meat is browned, remove from the pan and transfer to a large, deep saucepan while you fry the onion until it is soft and golden.

Once the onion is cooked, add to the pan with the meat. Stir the black treacle, Worcestershire sauce and tomato purée into the hot water and stir it all into the meat and onion. Add the bay leaf, carrots and parsnips and season with pepper.

Bring everything to the boil, then turn down the heat and simmer for 2–3 hours until the gravy has thickened and the meat and vegetables are soft and succulent. Check and stir from time to time: you may need more liquid. Check for seasoning towards the end of the cooking time: you may need a little salt.

When the stew is almost ready, make the dumplings.

To make the dumplings
Put the suet into a bowl and sieve the flour over it, season with salt and pepper and mix to a fairly stiff dough with the water: a dinner knife is the ideal tool for this. Flour your hands and divide the mixture into 4 equal pieces and shape into balls between the palms of your hands. Each ball should be a fraction bigger than a ping-pong ball.

Lower the dumplings carefully into the stew using a tablespoon. They will sink, but don't worry: they will rise again as they cook. Put a lid on the pan and simmer for about 20 minutes until the dumplings have doubled in size and risen to the top of the stew. The lid needs to be on to build up steam inside the pan as the dumplings are cooked by a combination of simmering in liquid and steaming.

The stew needs to be simmering and bubbling but there is no need to have it heaving and boiling: the flavour of the stew will be spoilt and it can boil over or catch on the bottom.

Serve the stew and dumplings together, immediately, with mashed or plain boiled potatoes. If you have any wide soup plates they are useful to serve this in: the gravy is a little bit more soupy than usual in order to cook the dumplings.

For the dumplings
25g (1oz) suet
50g (2oz) self-raising flour
Pinch of salt
Black or white pepper, freshly ground
2–3 tablespoons cold water

NOURISHING BEEF CASSEROLE

This is a really easy, comforting dish: it is nice and warming on a cold winter's day. It's also useful in times of crisis when a square meal is called for, but nothing fancy that needs concentration to prepare and serve. If you can't face peeling and mashing potatoes you can bake some in the oven while the casserole is cooking instead.

SERVES 2–3 but it's easy to double up on quantities

450–500g (1lb) braising or preferably feather steak (ask your local butcher)
1 tablespoon plain flour
150 ml (¼ pint) stout
425ml (¾ pint) water
1 tablespoon Worcestershire sauce
1–2 tablespoons black treacle
1 tablespoon tomato purée
1 good-sized onion, sliced
2 or 3 carrots, peeled and cut slantwise, into wedges
150g (5 oz) mushrooms, sliced, or whole if small
1 bay leaf
Black or white pepper, freshly ground
A little oil for greasing

You will need a greased casserole dish with a lid

Preheat oven to 140ºC–150ºC (fan oven) or equivalent.

Cut the meat into cubes and toss in the flour. Alternatively, instead of cubes, cut the meat into two or three pieces and serve one piece per person.

If you would like to brown the meat first in hot oil for extra flavour, please do so but it will be perfectly fine if you just put it straight into the casserole dish. Add the stout and water, Worcestershire sauce, black treacle and tomato purée, the vegetables, and bay leaf. Season lightly with pepper. Cover and put in the oven, checking and stirring occasionally, for about 3 hours, or until everything is beautifully cooked and succulent. Test and adjust the seasoning, you may like to add a little salt.

Serve with plenty of mashed potatoes or baked potatoes.

Beef in Stout with Redcurrant Jelly

This is an equally delicious variation of the above recipe. Instead of the Worcestershire sauce, black treacle and tomato purée, add **a generous tablespoon of redcurrant jelly** instead.

Magic Jam Stew

This is a really unusual recipe! You wouldn't think there could possibly be enough liquid for the meat to cook in, but somehow there is. It is also exceptionally easy to make and has very few ingredients.

Preheat oven to 140ºC (fan oven) or equivalent.

Cut the meat into cubes. Put it straight into a greased casserole dish. Peel the apple and dice it into fairly small pieces as you want it to cook right down. Add it to the meat and stir in the jam and curry paste or powder. Cover tightly (if your dish has no lid, use foil) and put it into the oven and cook gently for 2–3 hours.

Check after an hour or so and give it a good stir. If it seems a bit dry you can add a little water, or a spot of apple juice, but not too much. Before serving, taste and add a little salt if necessary.

Serve with plenty of mashed potatoes, or rice if you prefer.

Variation
Apricot conserve goes very nicely with the apple and curry flavours. Also, if you add a handful of sultanas halfway through the cooking time, you have a lovely old-fashioned tasting dish of beef curry.

SERVES 2 but you can easily double it

Roughly 500g (1lb) good braising steak, or preferably feather steak if you can get it (see your local butcher)
1 large cooking apple or 2 smaller eating apples
1 tablespoon of a fairly tart jam or jelly such as: plum, damson or crab apple jelly
1 teaspoon curry paste or curry powder to taste
Possibly a little salt to taste

BEEF WITH PICKLED WALNUTS

This is a gorgeous warming casserole for winter nights. It reheats brilliantly. Serve with plenty of mashed potato to soak up the gravy. If you have any left over (as if), it makes a good quick lunch or supper with egg noodles. Pickled walnuts may sound like a strange ingredient for a casserole but they add the most fantastic flavour. Keep a jar to hand and add the liquid, or some of the walnuts, finely chopped, to stews and gravies.

SERVES 4–6

900g (2lb) or so of
  braising steak, or ideally
  feather steak (see your
  local butcher)
450g (1lb) or so of carrots
3–4 onions
2 tablespoons flour
Mild olive oil
4–6 pickled walnuts, cut
  into pieces, and 2
  tablespoons of liquid
  from the jar
570ml (1 pint) or so hot
  water or vegetable
  cooking water
2 bay leaves
Freshly ground black
  pepper
225g (8oz) roughly of
  mushrooms

Cut the meat into chunks, peel and slice the carrots diagonally, peel and slice the onions. Toss the meat in the flour. Heat the oil in a wide pan and fry the meat until lightly browned. Next, put all the browned meat and vegetables back in the pan and add the walnuts and their liquid, the hot water, the bay leaves and a good grinding of pepper, and stir everything together thoroughly. Bring to the boil and then simmer gently for about 3 hours until everything is tender and the gravy has thickened. About 2 hours into the cooking time, add the mushrooms, sliced if large or whole if small. Check and stir from time to time. Check for seasoning before serving, you may need a touch of salt.

If you prefer, after browning, you can transfer everything to a greased, covered casserole dish and cook in a preheated oven for about the same amount of time, at 150ºC (fan oven) or equivalent. Again, check and stir from time to time.

If you are very short of time to prepare, leave out the browning stage and put the floured meat and vegetables straight into the greased casserole dish.

LIVER AND BACON WITH A RICH ONION GRAVY

This is a lovely hearty plateful for dreary winter days. Don't overcook the liver or have the heat too high; you want it to be soft and succulent.

Start the gravy first of all. Slice the onion and fry in a tablespoon or two of oil until soft and golden. Stir in a rounded tablespoon of flour and cook, still stirring, for a minute or two. Spoon the black treacle, Worcestershire sauce and tomato purée into a jug and top up with the hot water and stir. Add to the onion and flour gradually, stirring constantly. Bring to the boil, reduce the heat to moderate and simmer for an hour or so, stirring from time to time. Add a little more water or vegetable cooking water if it seems too thick.

About half an hour before you are going to eat, dust the liver with the rest of the flour and a good grinding of pepper. Heat a little oil in a pan and fry the liver gently, over a moderate heat, for around 15–20 minutes or until cooked through but still a fraction pink inside.

Cut most of the fat from the bacon using sharp kitchen scissors and cut each rasher into 4 pieces. Fry in a little hot oil (you can fry it with the liver if your pan is big enough) until it is just verging on slightly crispy.

About 10 minutes before you are ready to eat, tip the bacon and liver into the gravy to finish cooking and for the flavours to amalgamate.

Serve with plenty of mashed potatoes and vegetables: peas seem to go well, as do baby carrots. A dab of mustard would also be welcome.

SERVES 2–3

I large onion
Mild oil for frying
2 tablespoons plain flour: I for the gravy, I to coat the liver
2 tablespoons black treacle
I tablespoon Worcestershire sauce
I teaspoon tomato purée
Approximately 425ml (¾ pint) hot water
225–350g (½–¾lb) lamb's liver
Freshly ground black or white pepper
3–4 rashers of back bacon

SHEPHERD'S PIE

*This is one of three different versions of shepherd's pie. There is this one, made with **mince**; another plainer, more nursery type version made with **leftover lamb or beef,** in the Roast Dinners section; and a chilli version made with **leftover chilli, topped with grated cheese** (page 76). All are very nice indeed and all seem to need a little spot of tomato ketchup on the side.*

SERVES 4

Approximately 450g (1lb)
   lean minced beef (or
   lamb)
1 large onion
2–3 carrots
1 stick celery, plus celery
   leaves if possible
150g (5oz) mushrooms
1 tablespoon plain flour
1 tablespoon black treacle
275ml (½ pint) hot water
1 tablespoon
   Worcestershire sauce
1 tablespoon tomato purée
   (or tomato ketchup in an
   emergency)
1 bay leaf
Freshly ground black or
   white pepper
A couple of handfuls of
   frozen peas (optional)
2–3 tablespoons oil
Salt to taste

About 1–1½ kilos (3lb)
   potatoes
Butter for mashing and
   dotting on top

If you have two large frying pans it is helpful. Brown the mince: if you start it off slowly you may not need oil, otherwise use a small amount.

Slice the onion and cook in the other pan with the oil, until soft and golden. Peel and slice the carrots fairly finely, slice the celery and celery leaf finely and cook in the pan with the onion. Slice the mushrooms; if you are able to get the type with open gills, they will help to colour the mince nicely. Add the mushrooms to the other vegetables and continue cooking until soft.

Stir the flour into the mince once it is browned. Spoon the treacle into the hot water and stir to dissolve. Pour into the mince mixture with the Worcestershire sauce, tomato purée and bay leaf. Add the vegetables and season with pepper. Stir everything together and simmer for 1–2 hours until everything is fully cooked and the flavours have mingled.

Stir occasionally and add a little more water or, better still, cooking water from the potatoes, if it seems a bit dry, but bear in mind you don't want it to be too sloppy or it will boil out of the pie once it is in the oven. If you are using peas, add them towards the end of the cooking time; if you add them too early they will lose their bright vibrant colour.

Meanwhile, cook the potatoes in the usual way and mash with butter. If they are very stiff, loosen with a little hot milk or potato cooking water.

Check the mince for seasoning: it may need a touch of salt. Put it into an ovenproof dish and top with the mashed potato. Make a pattern in the potato with a fork (the ridges will help the top crisp nicely), dot with butter to aid browning further, and bake in a moderate oven (180ºC, fan oven, or equivalent) for approximately 20 minutes or until the top is golden. You may like to stand the dish on a baking tray in case anything does boil over.

Serve with crusty bread and a green vegetable.

SAVOURY MINCE

Instead of making a shepherd's pie you can serve the mince and potatoes separately. If you do this, it's nice to top the mince with a few **croutons** or triangles of **fried bread**. Heat some **oil** in a frying pan, turn the heat down to moderate and fry little squares or larger triangles of bread on both sides until crisp and golden.

LAMB HOTPOT

This is another nourishing winter dish. This isn't strictly the same as the traditional Lancashire Hotpot as the meat is off the bone and there are no lamb's kidneys, which are often part of the traditional version. The meat is laid on top of the vegetables and the potatoes are in a single layer on top, rather than layered throughout in the usual way. Also, it contains pearl barley, which isn't normally included but gives extra nourishing body and flavour.

You will need a large greased casserole dish with a lid.

Preheat oven to 150ºC (fan oven) or equivalent.

Trim any excess fat from the meat, dust it with flour and brown in the oil. Put the sliced onion and carrots, pearl barley and bay leaf into your casserole dish. Sit the browned meat on top. Discard the oil from the pan but scrape any lamby residue over the meat.

Cut the potatoes in half, rest each piece, cut side down, on a board and cut into thin slices.

Season the meat with black pepper and spoon the Worcestershire sauce and black treacle into a measuring jug and top up with the hot water. Pour over the meat and vegetables, layer the potato slices over the top.

Cover and cook for a good two hours or more or until everything is tender and melting and the liquid has reduced. Check from time to time, add more water if necessary or adjust the oven temperature if required.

Remove the lid for the last half hour of cooking to allow the top to brown. Check for seasoning before serving; you may need a touch of salt at the table.

Traditionally, Lancashire Hotpot is served with pickled red cabbage: this version goes very well with **Baked Red Cabbage,** a green vegetable and some crusty bread.

SERVES 2–4

450g (1lb) or a little more, neck or shoulder of lamb, off the bone, cubed

1 heaped tablespoon plain flour

Oil for frying

1 large onion, sliced

2–3 carrots, peeled and thinly sliced

25g (1oz) pearl barley

1 bay leaf

450g (1lb) potatoes or a little more, say 3 medium potatoes, peeled or scrubbed

Freshly ground black pepper

1 tablespoon Worcestershire sauce

1 tablespoon black treacle

425ml (¾ pint) hot water

LAMB WITH TOMATO SAUCE, BEANS AND HERBS

*This is quick, easy and delicious. Try it with **Roast Potatoes with Salt and Herbs** in the **Roast Dinners section** and a steamed green vegetable. The quantities given are approximate and depend on how many you are feeding. It is important that the lamb is soft and succulent, not overcooked and hard. Summer savory and winter savory are not generally available in the shops, but if you grow your own you may like to add some with the rosemary and thyme. Apart from having a lovely thymey flavour, both kinds of savory are meant to help with the digestion of beans!*

1–2 lamb steaks per person

A little oil for frying

Sprigs of rosemary and thyme

Approximately 4 tablespoons per person of **Easy Tomato Sauce for Pasta** (see page 71), or from a jar

Approximately 2 tablespoons per person of drained, tinned cannellini, flageolet or haricot beans (or a mixture)

A splash of red or white wine

Fry the lamb steaks in a little oil over a moderate heat, turning from time to time. You can grill them if you prefer, but try to reserve the juices. About halfway through the cooking time add the rosemary and thyme.

Meanwhile, pour the tomato sauce and beans into another pan and heat through. Once the lamb is almost cooked, remove from the pan, discard the herbs and add the wine to the juices. Keep stirring for a few moments, letting the wine bubble and scraping the bottom of the pan to loosen any flavoursome residue. Continue until the wine starts to look a little bit syrupy.

Return the lamb to the pan and add the tomato sauce and beans, heat together gently for a few moments or until you are ready to serve.

If you don't want to use wine, just scrape the bottom of the pan and move on to the next stage.

BELLY PORK WITH BLACK TREACLE AND BUTTER BEANS

This is a warming dish for a cold day. It goes beautifully with plenty of mashed potatoes to soak up the sauce or rice and steamed Chinese greens such as pak choi. You may want to cut the fat and rind off the pork slices but don't do it until after cooking as it helps to thicken and flavour the sauce.

A wide wok-style frying pan is useful for this recipe

Fry the pork until lightly browned on both sides. Remove from the pan and drain on kitchen paper, keep warm. Drain away any fat from the pan but scrape any porky residue from the bottom over the pork slices so that it is included in the finished dish.

Fry the onion and carrots until the onion is soft and golden and the carrots are slightly coloured. Remove from the pan and drain on kitchen paper.

Wash out the pan and return the onion and carrots. Stir the black treacle and tomato purée into the hot water and add to the pan.

Add the pork and beans, season with plenty of black pepper and bring to the boil. Turn down the heat and simmer gently for around two hours or until the sauce has thickened and reduced and the carrots are softened.

SERVES 2–4

- 4 slices of belly pork
- A little oil for frying
- 1 large onion
- 2–3 carrots, cut into diagonal slices
- 2 tablespoons black treacle
- 2 teaspoons tomato purée
- 425ml (¾ pint) hot water
- 420g tin of butter beans in water, drained
- Freshly ground black pepper

STEAK AND MUSHROOM PIE

This is a lovely rich beef casserole topped with a puff pastry lid. It's a great wintertime family meal, special enough for Sunday lunch or when you have guests. Serve with hearty helpings of mashed or boiled potatoes and steamed broccoli, carrots and cauliflower with a little mustard on the side. Don't worry about the pickled walnuts: they are a bit like anchovies in that they look scary but melt away to nothing, leaving behind a beautiful rich flavour and depth.

SERVES 4

450g (1lb) braising steak or preferably feather steak (ask your local butcher)

1–2 tablespoons plain flour

Mild oil for frying

1 large onion, sliced

150g (5oz) mushrooms, closed cap, button or chestnut, sliced or whole if small

Approximately 570ml (1 pint) hot water

1 bay leaf

Freshly ground black pepper

1–2 pickled walnuts and 2 tablespoons of liquid from the jar

225g (8oz) ready-made puff pastry

You will need a 2 pint pie dish with a flat rim and a pie funnel or a greased baking tray

Cut the steak into bite-size pieces, removing any excess fat, and coat in the flour. Heat the oil in a wide pan and brown the meat on all sides. Fry the onion in hot oil in another pan until soft and golden, add the mushrooms once the onion is nearly cooked.

When the meat is browned, stir in the hot water, and keep stirring for a few moments. Add the onion and mushrooms, the bay leaf and a good grinding of black pepper. Slice the pickled walnut(s) very finely and add to the pan with the liquid from the jar. Stir everything together thoroughly and bring to the boil. Turn the heat down to a simmer and cook for approximately 2 hours, stirring from time to time and adding more water if necessary, until the meat is tender and the sauce has reduced and thickened.

Once the meat is nearly cooked, preheat the oven to 200–220°C (fan oven) or equivalent. Refer to the pastry manufacturer's instructions and be guided by them as you assemble and bake the pie.

To Make the Pie: Method 1

Cut out the pastry generously to fit over your pie dish, using the upturned dish as a guide. Pour the steak and mushrooms into the dish and settle the pie funnel in the middle. Lightly grease the rim of the dish and pick up the pastry, draping it over your rolling pin. Manoeuvre it over the pie dish and ease into position over the top of the pie funnel so that the funnel pokes through. Firm the edges gently with your fingertips or the back of a fork.

Don't stretch the pastry *at all*: if you do, it will ping away from the sides of the dish like elastic and fall into the filling during cooking!

Method 2

Cut out individual circles, squares or triangles for each person and bake on a greased baking tray, following the manufacturer's instructions. To serve: spoon the steak and mushrooms onto each serving plate and sit a pastry lid on top. This method is especially useful if you want to double the quantity as it is easier than making two complete pies.

You may like to glaze the top of the pastry with beaten egg for a really glossy, professional finish but it looks beautiful without.

See the **Pastry** section for **Steak and Potato Pie.**

CREAMY CHICKEN AND MUSHROOMS

This makes a lovely savoury dish to serve with mashed potatoes, or rice if you prefer. You can use chicken breasts or leftover cooked chicken.

SERVES 2–4

2 chicken breasts or
   leftover chicken
A little oil
1–2 leeks
Approximately 150g (5oz)
   mushrooms, closed cap,
   chestnut or a mixture of
   both
1–2 carrots, thinly sliced
   (or a handful of frozen
   baby carrots)
415g tin of luxury
   mushroom soup
A little freshly ground
   black pepper
Approximately 75g (3oz)
   frozen sweetcorn

Fry the chicken breasts, turning from time to time, for 20–30 minutes until completely cooked. Meanwhile, in a separate pan, gently fry the leeks and mushrooms for a few moments until they are both beginning to soften.   Add the carrots and stir in the soup and black pepper. Stir thoroughly and simmer. Once the chicken has cooked, add to the soup mixture and continue to simmer for about an hour or so or until the soup has reduced and thickened and the flavours have amalgamated. Add the sweetcorn for the last 20 minutes or so of cooking time.

If you are using leftover chicken, add halfway through the cooking time: bring the soup to boiling point, stir thoroughly and cook for a few moments, then turn the heat to a simmer and continue to cook as before.

This also works well with leftover turkey.

CHICKEN AND MUSHROOM PIE

The previous chicken recipe works beautifully as a pie filling. You will need **225g (8oz) ready-made puff pastry**. You can put your filling in a pie dish and roll out a top to fit and bake as a pie, or you can roll out individual circles or squares, bake them on a greased baking tray and position them on top of the creamy chicken on individual plates as you serve. See Steak and Mushroom Pie, above.

LIGHTLY CURRIED CHICKEN SUPPER

You can use chicken breasts or leftover cooked chicken for this lightly curried dish. Plain rice is the most usual choice to serve with it but it is also great with mashed potatoes topped with a little onion fried until it is almost crispy.

Fry the chicken breasts, turning from time to time, for 20–30 minutes until completely cooked. Meanwhile, in a separate pan, fry the onion until soft and golden, stir in the curry paste and cook for a few moments. Add the soup and sultanas, if using, stir thoroughly and simmer. Once the chicken has cooked, add to the soup mixture and continue to simmer for an hour or so or until the soup has reduced and thickened and the flavours have amalgamated.

If you are using leftover chicken, add halfway through the cooking time: bring the soup to boiling point, stir thoroughly and cook for a few moments, then turn the heat to a simmer and continue to cook as before.

This also works well with leftover turkey.

Reheating cooked meat
When reheating any leftover cooked meat, be sure to cook it thoroughly until piping hot.

SERVES 2–4

2 chicken breasts or
   leftover chicken
A little oil
1 large onion
1 level dessertspoon curry
   paste, such as Madras
   (or to taste)
415g tin of luxury
   mushroom soup
Handful of sultanas
   (optional)

Sausages and Mash

This has got to be one of the great high spots of the British winter menu! You need to buy really decent butcher's quality sausages: nothing bland and pasty of dubious origin. You need plenty of smooth and fluffy mashed potatoes and beautiful rich gravy with maybe a selection of mustards. Below are some tips and serving suggestions rather than an actual recipe.

Try cooking your sausages in a baking dish in a preheated oven at 180ºC (fan oven) or equivalent for about 20 minutes, turning halfway. It is much easier this way: the cooking is nice and even, the sausages cook thoroughly on the inside and you get a gorgeous sticky residue on the outside. With grilling and frying you need to watch them constantly and it is difficult to judge the temperature precisely so that the inside is cooked and the outside isn't burnt and hard. Also, particularly with grilling, the sausages tend to spit all over the grill itself and the kitchen becomes full of the smell of burning fat. Horrible!

Once the sausages are cooked, take them out of the oven and prick them carefully with the point of a sharp knife. Sausages usually contain a fair bit of fat but if you prick them before cooking they will be very dry and not as tasty. Do this at arm's length and take care as the fat can spurt out quite a long way! Finally, sit the sausages on some kitchen paper for a few moments.

For perfect mashed potato: see the **Roast Dinners** section.

Champ is also *completely wonderful* with sausages: see the **Roast Dinners** section.

For perfect gravy, see the **Liver and Bacon** recipe above and also **Proper Home-Made Gravy** in the **Roast Dinners** section.

SAUSAGES WITH CHILLI AND MARMALADE SAUCE

This may sound a bit unusual but it is another great sausage dish! Sausages and marmalade work strangely well together and the chilli and marmalade are also good, if unlikely sounding, partners.

Preheat oven to 180°C (fan oven) or equivalent.

Cook the sausages in an ovenproof dish in the oven for around 20 minutes or until nicely browned. Prick as in Sausage and Mash recipe above.

Slice the chilli into a small saucepan and cook briefly in a little oil until just soft. Stir in the marmalade and orange juice and cook over a moderate heat, stirring constantly, until the marmalade has melted and combined with the juice. Pour into a jug and hand round at the table.

Serve with mashed potatoes and steamed green beans. You might like to mash the potatoes with a little garlic or, alternatively, a little crème fraiche or some cream cheese instead of butter and hot milk.

SERVES 2–3

6–8 good-quality sausages
I red chilli (or half, depending on personal taste)
A little oil
2 generous tablespoons marmalade
The juice of half an orange (or 2 tablespoons of juice from a carton)

SAUSAGES AND BACON WITH TOMATOES AND BEANS

*You can make a big saucepan of this for Bonfire Night to serve with baked potatoes or crusty bread: slice the sausages to make them go further and make them easier to eat if people are standing up. Alternatively, it makes a hearty supper served with **Roast Potatoes with salt and Herbs**: see the **Roast Dinners** section.*

SERVES 4–8 but it's easy to double quantities

1 large onion
1–2 tablespoons oil
1 red chilli
2 400g tins tomatoes
2 tablespoons black treacle
2 heaped teaspoons wholegrain mustard
Freshly ground black pepper
A few sprigs of thyme and a little summer or winter savory, if available
A 400g tin each of haricot and cannellini beans, drained (or same amount of other similar beans)
2 bay leaves
225g (½lb) bacon (back or streaky, green or smoked) cut into bite-size pieces
6–8 butcher's quality sausages

Slice the onion and fry in the oil until soft and golden. Add the chilli towards the end of the cooking time. Empty the tomatoes into a bowl, slice them roughly with a knife and then mash them with a fork, removing any bits of skin and central core, including as many seeds as possible. Add the tomatoes to the pan with the onions and chilli and add the black treacle, mustard, black pepper, herbs, beans and bay leaves. Stir everything thoroughly together and bring to the boil. Turn down the heat and simmer gently for around two hours until the sauce has thickened and reduced and the flavours have amalgamated. A spatter guard is useful.

When the sauce has been simmering for about an hour, fry the bacon until cooked but not yet crisp and bake the sausages in the oven, turning once, at 180ºC (fan oven) or equivalent for 20 minutes or until golden brown and cooked through. Remove from the oven and prick as described in the Sausage and Mash recipe above. Add the bacon and sausages to the tomato sauce for the last half hour of cooking. Check for seasoning. Alternatively, fry the bacon until crisp just before everything is ready, and scatter over the top of each serving.

QUICK CURRIED SAUSAGE SUPPER

This is quick and delicious: just the thing when you are tired and hungry after a long day.

Preheat oven to 180°C (fan oven) or equivalent.

Slice the onion quite thickly and fry in the oil until soft and golden and just starting to be tinged with brown. Stir in the curry paste and cook for a few moments. Pour in the soup, stir thoroughly and simmer over a moderate heat to reduce and thicken while you cook the sausages. Check and stir the soup from time to time.

Cook the sausages in the oven as in the previous sausage recipes. Once the sausages are cooked, remove from the oven and prick as before. Add to the pan with the soup and cook for a few minutes more so that the flavours can amalgamate.

Serve with rice or plenty of mashed potatoes and a green vegetable.

SERVES 2–3

1 large onion
A little oil
1 level dessertspoon curry paste, such as Madras (or to taste)
415g tin of luxury mushroom soup
6–8 good-quality sausages

Baked Red Cabbage

This is perfect with sausages, mashed or baked potatoes, green beans or broccoli and plenty of mustard.

1 red cabbage, roughly 500g (1lb) or a little more in weight
1 large onion
1 large cooking apple or 2 dessert apples, peeled and cored
A touch of garlic, if liked
2 level tablespoons unrefined granulated (or soft brown) sugar
A little salt and freshly ground black or white pepper
3 tablespoons red wine or cider vinegar
Knob of butter

You will need a greased casserole dish with a lid (if you have no lid, make your own from foil)

Preheat oven to 150°C (fan oven) or equivalent.

Remove any tough outer leaves from the cabbage and cut into quarters. Cut out the mid-ribs. Put each quarter, one at a time, flat side down and cut fairly thinly lengthwise. Cut across the slices once or twice as well so that people don't end up with long dangly pieces in their mouths! Slice the onion fairly finely and cut the apple into small chunks.

Put everything into the dish and mix together with your hands. Scatter a little garlic over the top, if using. Sprinkle the sugar, salt and pepper and vinegar over the top and give it a stir. Dot with butter and put the lid on. Cook for 2–3 hours: check and stir from time to time.

EASY TOMATO SAUCE FOR PASTA

This easy basic recipe can be used on its own over pasta or as a foundation for chilli, spaghetti bolognese, lasagne, moussaka or pizza topping. It is also suitable for young children. The following quantity is more than enough for two adults and you can easily make double.

Chop the onion fairly finely and cook in the oil over a medium heat until soft and barely coloured. Pour the tomatoes into a bowl and pick out any bits of stalk and skin and central cores: scoop out as many seeds as possible. Break up the tomatoes with a fork. Put into the pan with the onions.

Cook this over a low heat for an hour or so to reduce down, but if you are in a rush you could cook it more quickly, stirring frequently. In either case, a spatter guard is useful, as the tomatoes can spit a bit. Longer cooking makes a richer, thicker, jammier sauce, shorter cooking a fresher, lighter one.

Once the sauce is cooked, taste it and add a little sugar and/or salt if required. Usually no salt is needed but a little sugar might be. If this is for young children then definitely don't add salt and you may need to purée it.

This sauce is very plain and simple but you can easily add more flavours to it: add some finely sliced garlic or chilli with the onions; during the summer you can add some fresh herbs just before the end of the cooking time – basil and oregano are both particularly suitable. If no fresh herbs are available, and during the winter, dried oregano is a good substitute. A little finely sliced celery, including the celery leaves, also works well. You could also use a really decent extra virgin olive oil instead of a mild one.

You can freeze this very easily. Cool and pour into freezer bags or containers. It's useful to have a jar to hand in the fridge: a wide-necked jar makes a good container. It will keep for the best part of a week.

SERVES 2

1 onion
1 tablespoon of mild olive
  oil or rapeseed oil
2 400g tins of tomatoes
A pinch of sugar and/or, a
  pinch of salt, if required

SPAGHETTI BOLOGNESE

*Every family has their own recipe for this sauce, all much loved. This is a smooth, jammy, slow-cooked version with a good amalgamated texture to the sauce, no clumps of mince or chunky-style onions. Long, slow cooking makes a better dish. You don't **have** to add wine but it does contribute to the overall flavour and 'jamminess'. Serve with plenty of spaghetti.*

SERVES 4 but it's easy to
   double up on quantities

1 onion, finely sliced
1 finely sliced celery stalk,
   including leaf, plus as
   much extra leaf as
   possible
110g (4 oz) sliced
   mushrooms, button,
   closed cap or chestnut
Splash of olive oil,
   preferably extra virgin
1–2 cloves of garlic, finely
   sliced
450g (1lb) best-quality lean
   beef mince
Splash or two of red wine
   (optional)
400g tin of tomatoes
1 bay leaf
Freshly ground black
   pepper
Fresh basil or oregano, if
   available

Cook the onion, celery and mushrooms in the oil over a gentle heat: put a lid on the pan if you like. Once they have begun to soften, add the garlic and continue to cook until soft but not coloured. Brown the mince in a separate pan (drain off any excess fat if necessary). Add to the onion mixture and stir together. Pour in the wine, if using, and cook for a couple of minutes.

Break up the tomatoes and remove any bits of skin and central core, including as many seeds as possible. Add to the pan with the bay leaf and black pepper. Turn up the heat until everything is bubbling and then reduce the heat to moderate and simmer for an hour or more. If you are using fresh herbs, add them just a few minutes before you are ready to serve.

Serve with grated Cheddar cheese for an informal family meal or grated Parmesan or similar if you are entertaining or pushing the boat out. A few olives on top as well wouldn't go amiss.

✓ **Useful Note** Freeze any leftover wine if you have any (from the bottle, not people's glasses, obviously!) and use it for sauces and gravies. There is no need to defrost it first; it will melt quickly in the heat of the pan.

LASAGNE

Lasagne always seems a bit of a special meal: great for the weekend or if someone is coming round. Add a lovely big salad and some garlic bread and you are all set.

Preheat oven to 180°C (fan oven) or equivalent.

Make up the same quantity of bolognese sauce as above and include **1 red pepper, deseeded and sliced,** when you fry the onions.

Make a white sauce by mixing the cornflour with a little of the cold milk until it is smooth. Gradually incorporate the rest, stirring all the time. Bring to the boil, stirring very frequently, and keep stirring until it thickens. Remove from the heat and stir in most of the cheese.

Pour some cheese sauce over the bottom of your lasagne dish. Cover with the lasagne sheets: most standard dishes take two sheets side by side. Pour some of the bolognese sauce over, drizzle some more cheese sauce on top and cover with more lasagne sheets. You may have enough of the bolognese and cheese sauces for another layer but make sure you have enough cheese sauce left to cover the final layer of lasagne sheets completely. Finish off the top with the rest of the grated cheese. Put in the oven until the top is golden brown and bubbling.

SERVES 4

1 quantity of bolognese sauce, (see previous recipe)
1 red pepper, deseeded and sliced

2 heaped tablespoons cornflour
570ml (1 pint) semi-skimmed milk
110–150g (4–5oz) mature Cheddar cheese, grated

Ready-to-cook lasagne sheets, approximately 6 sheets (egg pasta is nicer)

GARLIC BREAD

A **French stick** or **baguette** makes the most traditional garlic bread but you can use **thick slices from an uncut white loaf** just as well. Cut your chosen bread into thick slices. Mix a **finely chopped clove of garlic or two** into some **softened butter** and butter the bread on both sides. Put the slices back together and wrap in foil. Bake in a moderate oven for 20–30 minutes. Turn off the oven and undo the foil, separate the slices slightly and leave in the cooling oven for a few minutes, with the door ajar for the steam to escape. If you prefer, you could make up your garlic butter with a little minced garlic from a jar.

HOME-MADE PIZZA: see pages 222–224.

CHILLI CON CARNE

The amount of chilli you use is a matter of personal taste. Adjust the quantity to suit yourself. Also it's a matter of personal preference whether you prefer chilli powder, dried chillies or fresh; all work well. If you are not sure how much to use, try between a quarter and half a teaspoon of chilli powder per 450g (1lb) mince to begin with and take it from there. Always include the cumin though, as this is key to the flavour.

SERVES 2–4 but it's easy to double quantities if you have a houseful

1 onion, finely sliced
1 green or red pepper, cored, deseeded and sliced
Splash of mild olive oil or rapeseed oil
1–2 cloves of garlic, finely sliced
½ teaspoon chilli powder or 1 finely sliced fresh red chilli
½ teaspoon ground cumin
450g (1lb) lean beef mince
400g tin of tomatoes
420g tin of kidney beans in water, drained and refreshed in cold water
1 bay leaf

Fry the onion and pepper in the oil until softened, add the garlic, chilli and cumin towards the end of cooking. Keep stirring and don't let the garlic burn or it will be bitter and horrible. In a separate pan, brown the mince on a low heat at first until the fat starts to render, then you can turn up the heat. If the mince is very lean you can add a little oil to help it along. Break up any lumps. Add the mince to the onion mixture. Break up the tomatoes and remove any bits of skin and central core, including as many seeds as possible. Add the tomatoes, beans and bay leaf to the mixture.

Turn up the heat until everything is bubbling then turn down the heat and simmer, if you can, for two to three hours, stirring from time to time. Add a splash of water if it looks too dry. Longer, slower cooking will always make a better chilli.

Grow your own chillies

Tiny, fiery chillies on small compact plants are easy to grow at home. They flower and fruit prolifically and look terrific on a sunny windowsill. The chillies mature from yellow, through orange to red, and at the end of the summer the plants are a riot of colour. Once they have matured, you can use them fresh from the plant, dry them, or freeze them. To freeze, just put them into a freezer bag and seal the top. There is no need to defrost: use from frozen and snip with scissors if you need to slice them. You will have enough chillies to last you all winter and beyond: three or four of these will make a lively chilli for four brave people.

Extras to serve with chilli

You might be having chilli for a family meal or you might have guests. You could serve it simply with plain boiled rice, crusty bread or a baked potato and a green salad, or you could be more ambitious and lay out a bit of a feast with bowls of **grated cheese**, **sour cream** and **taco chips** or a pile of **tortillas** and some of the following.

REFRIED BEANS

These are great but very filling: they also make a nice snack on their own with some toast.

Slice the onion thinly and fry in the oil until very brown and quite crispy. Remove from the pan and set aside on some kitchen paper. Add the kidney beans and mash roughly with a fork. Fry them in the oil used to cook the onions until heated through, turning frequently. If the mixture seems a bit dry, add a little water. Turn into a warmed serving dish and top with the onions.	I small onion Splash of oil 420g tin of kidney beans in water, drained and refreshed in cold water

GUACAMOLE

Guacamole recipes usually contain tomato: try this easy version without.

Slice and chop the onion *very* finely. You may not need to use all of it. Cut the avocados in half, remove the stones and scrape out all the flesh into a bowl. Try to include all the brightest green, most nutritious, bits from next to the skin. Mash to a purée with a fork and mix with the onion. Add the rest of the ingredients with a little salt, if liked. Try to make this as close to serving as possible as the avocado can discolour after a while.	½ a small onion 2 perfectly ripe avocados Juice of half a lemon (or a lime) A few drops of Tabasco or some finely chopped red chilli

TOMATO SALSA

This is a lightly cooked, rather than a fresh, salsa.

Fry the onion, pepper and chilli until soft but not coloured, remove any skin or central core from the tomatoes, including as many seeds as possible, and mash with a fork. Add to the pan with the rest of the ingredients and simmer until heated through. Serve hot or cold. **Useful Note** Avoid getting raw chilli all over your hands by using kitchen scissors instead of a knife to slice your chillies. Hold the chilli by the stalk end and cut straight into the pan. ✔ **Something extra special** Make a chilli using cubed braising or feather steak instead of mince. Preferably, make this the day before you want to eat it so the flavours can amalgamate and develop.	I small onion I green pepper (not too big) I small green chilli Splash of oil 400g tin of tomatoes I finely sliced garlic clove A few drops of Tabasco

CHILLI SHEPHERD'S PIE

If you do happen to have any chilli left over, it makes a fantastic shepherd's pie. In fact, you might like to make some chilli especially for it! Quantities depend on how much is left over.

Cook and mash some **potatoes**. Put the **leftover chilli** into an ovenproof dish and top with the potatoes. Make some lines across the top with a fork and cover with **grated cheese**. Bake in the oven at 180°C (fan oven) or equivalent until the chilli is heated through and the top is golden, melted and bubbling.

Serve with a green vegetable, some crusty bread and a little tomato ketchup.

MOUSSAKA

This is a really satisfying dish and special enough to share with friends. Traditionally, authentic moussaka is made with lamb but you can use beef instead for this home-cooked version if you like.

SERVES 4

1 onion, sliced
1 green pepper, cored, deseeded and sliced
Mild oil for frying
1–2 cloves of garlic, finely sliced
450g (1lb) lean lamb or beef mince
1 level teaspoon cinnamon, plus a little more for dusting
Good splash of red wine (optional)
400g tin of tomatoes, lightly mashed with a fork
2–3 tablespoons tomato purée
1 bay leaf
Freshly ground black pepper

You will need a greased ovenproof dish

Fry the onion and pepper in the oil until softened, add the garlic towards the end of cooking. Keep stirring and don't let the garlic burn or it will be bitter and horrible. In a separate pan, brown the mince over a moderate heat; if it is very lean you can add a little oil to help it along. Break up any lumps. Add the mince to the onion mixture, sprinkle the cinnamon over the top and stir it in. Add the wine and allow it to bubble for a couple of minutes. Add the tomatoes, tomato purée, bay leaf and black pepper.

Once everything is bubbling, turn down the heat and simmer for up to two hours, stirring from time to time. Add a splash of water if it looks too dry, although it shouldn't be too liquidy by the time you are ready to assemble the moussaka.

Once the mince mixture is almost ready to make up the moussaka, preheat the oven to 160°C (fan oven) or equivalent.

Slice the aubergine fairly thinly – no more than a centimetre thick – and fry on both sides in the oil over a moderately high heat until completely soft and lightly browned. Alternatively, brush with oil and grill. Sit the aubergine on kitchen paper for a few moments while you make the sauce.

Make a white sauce by mixing the cornflour with a little of the cold milk, in a heavy-bottomed saucepan, until it is smooth. Gradually incorporate the rest of the milk, stirring all the time. Bring to the boil, stirring constantly, and keep stirring until the sauce thickens. Remove from the heat and stir in the cheese. Put aside to cool slightly while you assemble the rest of the moussaka.

Check the mince mixture for seasoning – you may need a little salt – and put half into the casserole dish, cover with a layer of aubergine and add the rest of the mince. Finish with a layer of aubergine on top.

Beat the egg and egg yolk lightly and fold gently into the cooling sauce. Pour the sauce over the moussaka, dust lightly with cinnamon and bake for 20–30 minutes until the top is lightly golden.

Serve with crusty bread and a green salad. If you have people round you may like to serve a **Greek-style Salad – see Light Lunches and Midweek Suppers** – and some plain boiled rice as well.

A Word of Caution Don't have the sauce too hot when you add the egg, or the oven heat too high, or the enriched sauce will curdle and separate.

1–2 aubergines, weighing about 450g (1lb) in total

For the sauce
1 rounded tablespoon cornflour
275ml (½ pint) semi-skimmed milk
110g (4oz) mature Cheddar cheese, grated
1 egg and 1 egg yolk

POOR MAN'S MOUSSAKA

This is exactly the same as above, but use **sliced potatoes** (peeled or with skins left on) instead of aubergines. It is crucial that the potatoes are completely cooked and softened, so it is best to boil them first and allow them to cool before you slice them.

FISH PIE

Fish pie is such a great home-cooked dish. It is really adaptable, you can make it fairly economically or you can turn it into something a bit more luxurious with salmon and prawns, maybe even a bit of monkfish. You can make a plain white sauce or a cheesy one, or even a cheesy chilli one: they are all delicious.

This should serve 4 unless you are very hungry

900g–1kg 350g (2–3lb) cooked potatoes, mashed with butter and hot milk
2 rounded tablespoons cornflour
425ml (¾ pint) milk
150ml (¼ pint) double or single cream
Freshly ground white or black pepper
A few drops anchovy essence
150g (5oz) button mushrooms (anything with remotely open brown gills will stain the sauce a murky brown)
700–900g (1½– 2lb) firm fish such as cod, haddock: a mixture of plain and smoked fish is nice
Handful of prawns (optional)
Butter, for dotting over the top

Preheat oven to 180ºC (fan oven) or equivalent.

Prepare your mashed potatoes first of all and then make the white sauce.

Put the cornflour into a heavy-bottomed saucepan and add a little of the milk to make a smooth paste. Gradually add the rest of the milk, stirring all the time. Turn on the heat to full power and heat to boiling point, stirring all the time. Turn down the heat and simmer for a minute or two, still stirring. Remove from heat and stir in the cream and pepper. Finally, add the anchovy essence: add a little at a time and taste, as it's very salty.

Pour the sauce into a wide wok-style pan, large enough to give you room to manoeuvre. Slice the mushrooms fairly finely and stir into the sauce: there is no need to precook them. Cut the fish into bite-size pieces and add to the pan with the prawns, if using. Heat gently for the barest amount of time and stir as gently as possible otherwise the fish will break up and turn to an unidentifiable mush.

Turn it all into an ovenproof dish and cover with the mashed potato, smoothing it round the edges of the dish. Make wave patterns all over with a fork and dot with butter. Bake in the oven for about half an hour until it is browning nicely on top and fish and mushrooms are cooked through.

 Useful Note If the fish is frozen, cut it into pieces while it is only partly thawed as it's easier to cut neat pieces.

CHEESY FISH PIE AND CHEESY CHILLI FISH PIE

Both of these versions are lovely. For the cheese version make a cheese sauce by adding **110–150g (4–5oz) grated cheese** to the white sauce and leave out the anchovy essence. Instead of dotting the top with butter, sprinkle with **more cheese**. For the chilli version, soften a **sliced red chilli** in **a little oil** and add to the cheese sauce.

SEAFOOD PASTA

Also, any of these versions are great as a pasta dish. Instead of the potato topping, cook enough pasta for everybody: **pasta shells** look the part. Add some **cooked peas** and **sweetcorn** to the finished dish, which you may want to thin down a tiny bit with milk or cream, and you have a delicious seafood pasta.

SIMPLE WHITE FISH IN A CHEESE SAUCE

Alternatively, you might like to combine just a couple of the elements of a **Cheesy Fish Pie** together. Gently pan fry **cod or haddock fillet**, or a similar **white fish**, and make a **plain cheese sauce** to pour over it. Serve very simply with some fluffy mashed potato and peas, and maybe a little steamed broccoli.

CHICKEN SUPPER WITH TOMATOES AND PEPPERS

This is an easy supper to make and special enough for informal entertaining. Serve with either plain boiled rice and a steamed green vegetable or crusty bread and a salad. A few plump olives, black or green, scattered over the top, wouldn't go amiss. You might like to leave the skin on the chicken for this recipe, as it adds to the taste and texture. If you have any special olive oil, this could be a good time to use it: if you have a little oil separating from the sauce at the end, that's all to the good, as you can dip your bread in it.

SERVES 2 but it's easy to double or treble quantities

Oil for frying
2 chicken breasts
1–2 bell peppers, ideally 1 green and 1 red, yellow or orange, deseeded and sliced
Splash of wine, red or white
Sufficient **Easy Tomato Sauce for Pasta** for 2, or from a jar
Freshly ground black pepper
Salt to taste

Heat the oil in a pan and fry the chicken breasts for 20–30 minutes or until cooked through and golden brown.

Fry the peppers until soft. Add the wine to the pan and let it bubble for a while, add the tomato sauce and simmer until it has thickened and reduced. Check for seasoning, pour the tomato and pepper sauce over the chicken and cook together for a few minutes, until you are ready to serve.

Alternatively, instead of using tomato sauce you could slice and fry **1 small onion** until soft, with a little **finely sliced garlic**, add **a 400g tin of tomatoes**, breaking them up with a fork, and simmer until reduced.

FRIED CHICKEN WITH SECRET SPICES

This always seems such an American, yet homely, way to eat chicken: you can just picture well-scrubbed children in a log cabin sitting round a big table. You can make this with breadcrumbs or finely crushed cornflakes; both taste good. The ingredients are fairly approximate as the amounts depend upon the size of the chicken breasts. Once you have got the hang of this you might like to make up your own 'secret spices'.

Put the flour into a large polythene bag with the salt and spices and shake well. Cut the chicken breasts in two and put into the bag, one at a time. Give each one a good shake to coat, and flatten slightly, still in the bag, either with your hand or a rolling pin. Have the beaten egg ready in a dish.

If you are using breadcrumbs tear the bread into rough pieces and, using a food processor, whiz into fine crumbs. Tip into a dry frying pan (no oil) and heat on the hob over a moderate heat for a few minutes, stirring constantly with a wooden spoon or spatula. This is to dry out the crumbs and crisp them up a bit.

If you are using cornflakes put them onto one half of a clean dry tea towel, fold the other half over, and roll vigorously with a rolling pin until you have fine crumbs.

Once the crumbs are ready, tip them into a shallow dish and heat some oil in a frying pan over a moderate heat: you may need two pans.

Dip the floured chicken into the egg and then into the crumbs. Fry, turning from time to time, until the chicken is completely cooked and the coating is golden. Depending on the thickness of the chicken, this should take between 20 and 30 minutes. Sit the chicken on kitchen paper for a few moments to absorb any oil.

Serve with chunky chips, baked potatoes or mashed potatoes. Corn goes very well with fried chicken: corn on the cob, sweetcorn kernels, or creamed sweetcorn, if you can get hold of it, are all good.

SERVES 4

1–2 rounded tablespoons plain flour

About 1 teaspoon chilli powder

About 1 teaspoon ground cumin

About 1 teaspoon ground coriander

½–1 teaspoon salt

2 large chicken breasts, skins removed

1 egg, beaten with 1 teaspoon water

Either 25–50g (1–2oz) cornflakes or 75–110g (3–4oz) bread, preferably on the dry side

Oil for frying

CRISPY FISH

This is very popular with children and works well for a family meal. You can keep the fish in large pieces or cut it into small pieces or 'goujons'.

Quantities are approximate

SERVES 2–4

1–2 rounded tablespoons plain flour
About 450g (1lb) of firm white fish such as cod or haddock or similar
1 egg, beaten with 1 teaspoon water
Either 25–50g (1–2oz) cornflakes or 75–110g (3–4oz) bread, preferably on the dry side
Oil for frying

See **Fried Chicken with Secret Spices,** above, for how to prepare the cornflakes or breadcrumbs.

Put the flour in a shallow dish and coat the fish thoroughly. Have the beaten egg ready in a dish. Once the crumbs are ready, tip them into a shallow dish and heat some oil in a frying pan over a moderate heat: you may need two pans.

Dip the floured fish into the egg and then into the crumbs. Transfer to the hot pan, turn the fish over so that both sides are sealed in the hot oil and turn the heat down to moderate. Turn over from time to time until the fish is completely cooked and the coating is golden. This should take 15–20 minutes. Sit the fish on kitchen paper for a few moments to absorb any oil.

Serve with mashed or boiled potatoes, or chunky chips, and peas. Wedges of lemon, tartare sauce or a spot of mayonnaise or tomato ketchup would be welcome.

ROAST DINNERS

Roast dinners are the absolute pinnacle of home cooking for many people brought up in Britain. It is a combination of the actual food itself, the beautiful smells, the anticipation of a good feed, and the lovely cosy feeling of sitting down with the rest of the family and not having to rush.

Most cooks will say how easy and straightforward it is to cook a roast. Well, it is certainly straightforward but it's not *exactly* easy as there are so many components to get ready to bring to the table at the same time. Plus, a roast dinner is usually associated with Sundays and celebrations when the cook her- or himself would quite like to relax as well!

You just need to think things through before you start and perhaps consider cutting down on accompaniments and vegetables. It is better to give your full attention to larger amounts of fewer dishes.

Proper gravy is a must. Most people love roast potatoes and it is worth becoming a roast potato expert but mashed potatoes also work really well with a roast as they soak up all the lovely gravy and juices. Some families are huge Yorkshire pudding fans and feel beef isn't the same without it (or indeed any roast). It is well worth taking the time to perfect the art.

Beef

Serve with lots of lovely gravy, mashed or roast potatoes, Yorkshire pudding, and horseradish sauce or strong English mustard.

Pork

Serve with apple sauce and sage and onion stuffing and plenty of gravy. If you like crackling, rib of pork is the best cut. Ask your butcher to score it for you, and rub in plenty of salt before you put it into the oven. You might want to finish off the crackling by cutting it away from the joint and putting it into a separate dish and cooking it on its own for the last 20 minutes or so. Crackling shouldn't be tooth-breakingly hard: it should be crunchy and brittle like a good pork scratching.

Lamb and mutton

What is the difference between lamb and mutton? Without getting too technical, lamb comes from a young sheep less than a year old and, strictly speaking, mutton comes from a sheep more than a year old: quite often, it may have come from a two- or three-year-old sheep that has had two or three years' good grazing.

Lamb has a milder flavour, is more tender and has less fat. Consequently, it is more suited to shorter cooking times. Mutton has a greater depth of flavour and has developed more fat: it is perfect for long, slow cooking.

Serve lamb with mint sauce or mint jelly, redcurrant jelly and gravy. Mutton is good with all of these and also with onion sauce.

Chicken

Bread sauce, sage and onion stuffing, bacon rolls, sausages, cranberry sauce and mustard and gravy all go well with chicken. Try roasting it with something inside the cavity. Lemon or apple, an onion, or a head of garlic if you are a dedicated garlic lover, will all work well; they will give a subtle extra flavour and keep the inside moist.

Gammon

Some people are a bit dismissive about gammon and pineapple but they can make a lovely combination: the slightly salty, savoury gammon and the partly sour, partly sweet pineapple are great together, especially if you fry the pineapple in a little butter or oil or bake it in the oven until the edges are slightly browned and sticky. Sometimes a white sauce seems called for, poured over cooked carrots or cauliflower. Alternatively, cheese goes well with gammon: you could make a cheese sauce and serve it over cauliflower or steamed leeks.

Suggested cooking times for roasting meat

It is quite difficult to give definite times and temperatures for roasting meat. Ovens vary and different types and cuts of meat vary in density. Also, with beef and lamb, it depends on how well cooked you like it. The usual guide suggested is 20 minutes per pound or half kilo of meat, and 20 minutes over, but in practice this is usually not quite enough for most meat. You might be better thinking in terms of 25 to 30 minutes per pound, 25 to 30 minutes resting, and forget about the extra 20 minutes or so cooking time. As for temperature, you might roast meat at 180ºC if you have a really fierce fan oven: otherwise, you may be better at 190ºC or 200ºC or equivalent. Whatever temperature is best for your oven, always preheat it so that it is at the right temperature the moment the meat goes in.

Buy your meat from your local butcher and then you can ask his or her advice. They are the experts and you can learn a lot. After your butcher, trial and error is your best guide. Test your meat after the minimum cooking time: the juices should run clear when it is pierced by a sharp knife or skewer. Remember to test different parts of the joint as the meat may vary in density. Also, take the meat right out of the oven and close the oven door as soon as you can, otherwise you will lose your correct temperature. Once you get really good at this you might be able to tell when the meat is cooked just by the way it 'smells *right*'.

Cover any joint loosely with foil for most of the cooking time and remove it for the last half hour or so to brown. This is for two main reasons: first, so that your meat doesn't dry out; and, second, so that it doesn't spit fat all over the inside of the oven, which always makes the oven, and the kitchen (and you), smell absolutely terrible!

Finally, let the joint rest for the best part of half an hour before you carve it so the juices can settle back into the meat properly. If you don't do this, the meat will be fairly tough and not as succulent. Take it out of the oven and cover it loosely with foil again and keep it warm. This has the advantage of leaving space in the oven for something else such as Yorkshire puddings or a crumble.

Bone in? Bone out?

A joint of meat roasted on the bone will have a better flavour but a joint without a bone in will be easier to carve. It doesn't affect the cooking time massively except that the bone can sometimes conduct the heat a bit more efficiently to the centre so it cooks more evenly.

Carving

Even if you are no expert at carving you can make a fair go of it simply by bearing the following points in mind.

Make sure the meat is rested (see above); it will be much easier to carve.

Use a proper *sharp* carving knife and a proper long-handled carving fork. You can't slice properly with a blunt knife; you can only hack away at the meat.

Put the meat onto a flat board, preferably with a channel round the outside to catch the juices.

Now you have the correct tools and board, and the meat is rested, you are more than halfway there. As for the rest, approach it logically.

If you are carving a bird, remove the legs and wings, unless you are only carving half of it; in which case, remove the leg and wing on just one side. Now you can see what you are doing: take the skin off the breast and carve slices, keeping the knife parallel to the breast and cutting down towards the board.

You can serve the legs whole if it's a chicken; if it's a turkey, remove the skin and slice the meat from the legs as neatly as you can.

If you are carving a joint, spend a moment or two just looking at it to see the best angle to slice it. Again, cut down towards the board: never cut towards yourself. Also, put your fork in a position where you won't keep catching it with the knife, as you'll blunt the knife. Sometimes you can see the grain of the meat: if it is noticeable, slice along the lines of the grain.

EASY SUNDAY LUNCH FOR GUESTS WHEN TIME AND ENERGY ARE RUNNING LOW

This is a lovely easy and happily received informal lunch to make for guests. Roast a **chicken** with a **lemon** cut in half and some **herbs** in the cavity (or two chickens if you have a houseful). Buy or make two or three loaves of really good **bread** and make a big bowl of **salad**. Provide **butter** and **mayonnaise** and a **relish or two**, and put everything on the table with plates and knives and paper napkins. Make sure the table looks attractive and tempting. Ask one of your guests to carve and invite everyone to make their own sandwiches. Easy, delicious and relaxing!

HOT SUNDAY SANDWICHES

Sometimes there might not be time on a Sunday to cook a full dinner but you might feel you want to have a roast of some kind. What you can do is roast a joint of meat, forget about the vegetables and gravy and make some delicious hot sandwiches instead. Much as in the **Easy Sunday Lunch** previously, have some really good bread and a bowl of salad on hand: you could also add an extra accompaniment or two.

Hot Beef Sandwiches

Make sandwiches with horseradish sauce or hot English mustard. If you are fond of gherkins, have a bowlful of these as well.

Hot Pork Sandwiches

If you have the time to make some sage and onion stuffing balls, these are great sliced in the sandwich. If you can make some apple sauce as well, that would be perfect.

Hot Lamb Sandwiches

Make sandwiches with a touch of mint jelly or redcurrant jelly.

Hot Chicken Sandwiches

Again, some sage and onion stuffing balls would be good, and a little cranberry sauce would add the finishing touch.

PROPER HOME-MADE GRAVY

Conventionally, if you are having a roast, the gravy is made at the last minute, in the roasting tin. This is a bit of a tall order when you are trying to serve everything up and get everyone to the table at the same time. It's better to start your gravy an hour or so beforehand so you can get all the hard work out of the way in advance, give the flavours time to develop, and add the precious meat juices at the end. Also, right up until the time you add the meat juices the gravy is perfectly suitable for non meat eaters. It's also lovely with sausages or anything else where you would like gravy.

Slice the onion fairly finely and cook gently in the oil. A wide wok-style frying pan works perfectly for this.

Once the onion is softened and golden (not dark) brown, add the flour: sprinkle it over the onion and keep stirring for a few minutes, until the flour is absorbed. Next, put the Marmite and black treacle in a measuring jug, and top up with the hot water. Stir well and add it gradually to the onion, and keep stirring until smooth.

Bring to the boil then turn down the heat and simmer for a good hour; more if possible as the flavour gets better with longer cooking. Check and stir from time to time. If the gravy seems a little thick, add some more water or, better still, some cooking water from your vegetables.

Once you have your meat juices you can stir them in but skim off any fat first: a separator jug is good for this. If you do end up with a film of oil on top you can rescue the situation with several thicknesses of kitchen paper. Just press gently on top until all the fat is absorbed.

Sometimes you might like to add a spoonful of redcurrant jelly or something similar. A very little marmalade can work well and a generous spoonful of ginger marmalade is fantastic with sausages. If you want to add a slosh of wine or sherry, add it near to the beginning of the cooking time, so the flavour can mellow out.

Thick or thin gravy?
This is entirely a matter of personal taste so adjust it to suit yourself. If you have ever seen the film *Twister*, you might remember the aunt of one of the lead characters, whose gravy was described as 'practically a food group in its own right'. Now that is something to aspire to!

See also **Liver and Bacon with a Rich Onion Gravy** recipe.

Ingredients

1 onion
Approximately 2 tablespoons mild flavourless oil
1 heaped tablespoon plain flour
1 teaspoon Marmite
1 generous teaspoon black treacle
425–570ml (¾–1 pint) hot water

Individual Yorkshire Puddings

Little individual Yorkshire puddings have become really popular in recent years and it is generally agreed that smaller Yorkshire puddings rise more easily. The following recipe is for a smaller than usual amount of batter for 12 small individual puddings.

*The idea of Yorkshire pudding originally was to eat it **before** the meat, possibly with a little gravy. This filled you up and then you didn't mind not having very much meat, which was (and still is) expensive.*

*Here are some crucial tips for Yorkshire pudding success: **the most essential tip is that the fat and the oven both need to be very hot**. Also, the batter needs to be at room temperature and the consistency of thin cream. Don't open the oven door during cooking, and once cooked, get them to the table immediately because they will start to taste a bit leathery after a while.*

Some people swear by half milk, half water but possibly this comes from the days when the only milk available was full cream. Once you get to the stage where you are taking the hot fat out of the oven be doubly sure you have cleared any animals and children from the area and protect your hands and arms well with oven gloves!

50g (2oz) plain flour
1 egg, as fresh as possible
150ml (¼ pint) semi-skimmed milk
Pinch of salt
Beef dripping from the joint if you have any, otherwise use oil

You will need an ordinary 12-cup tart tin

Preheat the oven to 220ºC (fan oven) or equivalent.

Sieve the flour into a bowl, make a well in the middle, add the egg and stir with a large dinner fork until combined and then add the milk gradually, always stirring it in thoroughly before you add more, until you have a thin batter, the consistency of thin cream. Stir in the salt. Finish mixing with a coiled spring type whisk. Leave to stand for 10–30 minutes at room temperature.

Put a little dripping or oil into the tin and put it into a hot oven until a slight haze rises from it. Give the batter a final whisking and transfer it into a jug with a good pouring spout. Take the tin out of the oven and put it onto a solid surface. Close the oven door immediately to keep the heat in. Working quickly (but carefully), divide the batter equally between the 12 cups. If the batter sizzles and hisses as it hits the fat, you will know you are on to a winner! Get the puddings back into the oven without delay and cook for 10 minutes or until they are well risen, puffed up and golden.

✓ **Oven Note** It is at times like these that you realise how essential it is to keep your oven scrupulously clean: if you don't, cooking Yorkshire puddings can be a bit of an eye-watering experience!

WHITE SAUCE

It is much easier to make a sauce this way, using cornflour, rather than make a roux with butter and wheat flour. The sauce is lovely and smooth, too.

Using a heavy-bottomed milk saucepan, mix the cornflour and a little of the milk to a smooth paste. Gradually add the rest of the milk, stirring as you add. Turn on the heat and bring to boiling point, stirring all the time. Turn down and simmer for a minute or two, stirring constantly.	2 heaped tablespoons cornflour 570ml (1 pint) semi-skimmed milk Freshly ground black or white pepper

CHEESE SAUCE

This is exactly the same as above, but add a **generous pinch of dry mustard** to the cornflour before you mix it with the milk and, once the sauce has thickened, remove it from the heat and stir in **175–225g (6–8oz)** of **grated Cheddar cheese**. See **Macaroni Cheese** and **Cauliflower Cheese**.

ONION SAUCE

This is lovely with lamb or mutton. Make a white sauce as above. Soften **a chopped onion** in **butter** and stir the softened onion into the white sauce. Season with **a little salt** to taste and some **freshly ground black or white pepper**.

BREAD SAUCE

Bread sauce is traditionally made with an onion spiked with cloves but try this version: it's delicious.

Slice the onion lengthwise and then cut the other way so that most pieces are about a centimetre square. Cook gently in the butter. The onion should be soft but barely coloured.	1 onion, peeled Knob of butter Roughly a third of a decent white loaf
Crumble the bread, inside only, not the crusts, over the top. Gradually pour the milk over the top, until all the bread has absorbed the milk and it is the consistency of porridge. Add a bit more bread if necessary.	275ml (½ pint) semi-skimmed milk Freshly ground white pepper
Season with about half a dozen twists of white pepper and simmer gently until hot throughout. You can make this ahead and reheat later if you like. It's also lovely cold with cold cuts and unexpectedly good hot with sausages.	

HOME-MADE SAGE AND ONION STUFFING BALLS

It's very easy and satisfying to make your own stuffing.

175–225g (6–8oz) brown bread: wholemeal or wholegrain, preferably not completely fresh 1 small white onion 40 fresh sage leaves or 2 heaped teaspoons dried sage 150ml (¼ pint) hot water (you may not need all of it) 1 egg, beaten (optional) Touch of salt and freshly ground white pepper Mild olive or rapeseed oil	Preheat oven to 180°C (fan oven) or equivalent. Tear up the bread and process in a food processor until you have fine breadcrumbs. Slice the onion into the thinnest, skinniest possible slices and cut crossways to make pieces approximately ½ cm long. Chop the sage finely if you are using fresh. Put the breadcrumbs into the largest frying pan you have and cook over a low to medium heat for a few minutes, stirring all the time with a wooden spoon until lightly toasted: you are aiming to dry them out rather than toast them. Combine the breadcrumbs, onion and sage together and stir in the hot water a little at a time. You may not need all of it, leave the mixture slightly dry if you are adding an egg. If you are using an egg (it is much nicer with, as is packet stuffing), allow to cool slightly before stirring the egg in and season lightly with salt and pepper. Pour a little oil in the bottom of your baking dish and put it into the oven to heat through. Wet your hands and shape the mixture into balls about half as big again as a ping-pong ball. Put them into the prepared baking dish carefully, turning them over in the hot oil so they are all coated. Bake for approximately 20 minutes.

✓ **Useful Note** Sliced onion freezes really well. Sometimes, if you are in a bit of a rush, it can be quite a fiddle to peel and slice an onion so it's useful to have some on hand in the freezer. Just peel and slice the onion as usual and tie securely into a freezer bag, and flatten it as much as possible before you put it in the freezer. Then, once you take it out again, it will defrost quickly. This is also useful for the times you have half an onion left over: if you put it in the fridge, the smell will permeate through everything else in there and you may not even get round to using it. Slice and freeze it instead.

ROAST POTATOES

Perfect roast potatoes are not easy to achieve. You really need to pay full attention as a few moments' under- or overcooking can spoil them completely. Points to bear in mind are: you need floury, not waxy, potatoes; the oil needs to be hot before you add the potatoes; and the potatoes need to be partly cooked before you put them in the oven, plus the outsides need to be a little bit roughed up so they will get nice and crispy.

Please bear in mind that you will be dealing with hot fat so clear the area of small children and animals and make a space near the cooker to put the hot dish on so that you are not traipsing across the kitchen with a dish of hot fat. Also, once you have drained the partly cooked potatoes, rest them on a clean tea towel for a few moments so that they are completely dry. If you try to put wet potatoes into the hot fat it will spit and if it catches you on the wrist or arm it really hurts! Roast them in a preheated oven at 180°C (fan oven) or equivalent.

ROAST POTATOES IN A HURRY

Having advised you to partially cook the potatoes first, actually you can roast them without doing this if you are in a rush. They are still nice but not *fabulous*! Preheat your oven to 180°C (fan oven) or equivalent. Cover the bottom of your roasting dish with oil and put into the oven to heat. Meanwhile, peel and cut your potatoes into halves or quarters. Again, you must dry them with a tea towel to prevent spitting. Roast until they are golden brown and soft inside.

Roast Potatoes in a Desperate Hurry with Added Health Benefits
As above, but just give them a good scrub and leave the skin on.

ROAST POTATOES WITH SALT AND HERBS

These are good with or without the skin left on. Cut the potatoes into bite-sized pieces – no need to cook them first – and put them into a roasting dish with some hot oil, as above. A ceramic dish is best as the pieces are small and can easily burn in a metal one. Scatter some flakes of Maldon Salt and some herbs such as sage, thyme and rosemary over the top. Cook as above but bear in mind that as they are cut smaller they will be ready much sooner.

BOILED POTATOES AND NEW POTATOES

There is an old adage that goes something like this: if something grows above ground, add boiling water to cook it; if it grows below ground, add cold water and bring it to the boil. This is generally sound advice. Occasionally, though, you might cook just a couple of servings of potatoes in the microwave, and in this case add boiling water.

For plain boiled potatoes: peel and cut into even-sized pieces, about the size of a small egg. Bring to the boil and simmer for 20–25 minutes or until tender. You don't actually need salt at this stage. If you are cooking new potatoes, scrub them lightly and if they are small enough cook them whole. Test after 10 minutes as they cook more quickly.

MASHED POTATOES

For perfect smooth mashed potatoes you really need a potato ricer. Cook as for boiled potatoes above and drain. Push the potatoes through the ricer and add a knob of butter and a little hot milk. You can heat the milk in a mug in a microwave if you have one: roughly a quarter of a mugful, heated on High for about 30 seconds, is about right for potatoes for four people. Beat the milk and butter in with a wooden spoon for a really smooth finish and season to taste.

Alternatively, you can use a potato masher, or a dinner fork, and then beat in the butter and milk with a wooden spoon, as above. If you don't want to use a lot of butter or milk, you can save a little of the cooking water and stir that in instead; it gives a light, smooth result. Be sure to choose a floury potato for mashing; the more waxy varieties don't mash at all well, they become very gluey and gloopy.

CHAMP

This is a traditional Irish way with mashed potatoes. Prepare and slice a bunch of spring onions, including some of the more tender green parts. Cook them gently over a low heat in a little butter until they are soft. Mash the potatoes with hot milk as above and stir in the onions and butter, season with pepper and a touch of salt if required. Champ is great with sausages or just on its own, eaten from a bowl with some extra very cold butter: make a hollow in the potato and slip the butter into it, then stir it through: there's nothing like it on a cold night!

Roast Parsnips with Honey and Mustard

These are always a popular part of a winter roast. For every **225g (½lb) of peeled parsnips** mix **1 tablespoon of runny honey** and ¼ **teaspoon of ready-made English mustard** together in a flat dish. It can be quite difficult getting the honey and mustard to stick to the parsnips and it helps if you warm the honey and mustard mixture briefly in the microwave for 20 seconds on High. Cover the bottom of a roasting dish thinly with **oil** and put in the oven to heat while you roll the parsnips in the honey and mustard. If the parsnips are small leave them whole, if they are large cut them into sections. Lower them carefully into the hot oil, spooning any honey mixture left in the dish over them. Bake at 180°C (fan oven) or equivalent, for about 30 minutes, turning halfway through cooking, until they are golden brown with appealingly sticky edges and completely cooked through.

Alternatively, instead of ½ teaspoon of strong English mustard use **1 teaspoon** of milder **wholegrain** or **Dijon mustard**.

Roasted Butternut Squash

Butternut squash is gorgeous roasted and very simple to do. Put some oil in the bottom of your dish and put it into the oven to heat. Peel the squash and remove the seeds. Cut into bite-sized pieces. Put them into the hot oil and turn carefully until they are coated. Bake for half an hour to an hour or until the corners are starting to brown and go a little bit sticky. They have the most beautiful flavour just as they are but occasionally you might like to scatter a few sage and thyme leaves over them before they go into the oven.

Steamed Broccoli

Broccoli is the most beautiful vegetable but not if it is overcooked: then it has that horrible sulphurous taste and smell and all the sweet nuttiness is lost. Steaming is the best way to cook it: it keeps its lovely bright green colour this way as well. Three minutes is usually all it takes in a steamer.

Cauliflower

You can boil cauliflower but again, like broccoli, it steams really well. About eight minutes in a steamer is about right.

CABBAGE AND KALE

Cabbage and kale are both really underrated. Just like broccoli and cauliflower, they steam really well. Shred them fairly finely, first discarding the tough outer leaves and mid-ribs.

Alternatively, shred them and stir-fry them in a little oil or butter for just a few minutes (they are also nice with a little bacon, cut into small pieces). Don't overdo it and 'stew' them though, or you are back to that horrible sulphurous taste and smell.

SPINACH

Wash briefly and steam for the briefest amount of time.

Alternatively, wilt gently in a pan with only the water still clinging to their leaves from washing, again for the briefest amount of time.

BRUSSELS SPROUTS

Try steaming these as well. Around five minutes is about right. (If freshly picked from the garden they may need less.)

CARROTS

You can boil carrots but they are better steamed, particularly if they are quite young. Depending on their age and size, steam for between five and eight minutes. If they are very big, slice lengthwise into quarters or diagonally into chunks. If you do boil the carrots, try to reserve the cooking water and use in gravy or soup: it will keep for a day or two, covered in the fridge.

PEAS AND BEANS

There is no doubt that peas picked fresh from the garden are best of all. You do need to cook them immediately though, or all the sugar turns to starch and they become tough and bullet-like. Frozen peas really are frozen within a very short time of picking so you are better with frozen peas than fresh ones that have been waiting around for too long. Try not to overcook your peas: for four servings they shouldn't really need more than three or four minutes, and the water should always be boiling to start with. Also, drain and serve them straight away: don't keep them hanging around in their cooking water.

You can cook green beans in water but again they are better steamed; they tend to hold on to water and it's difficult to drain it all away if they are actually cooked in water. Either way, cook them for about four minutes; they need to be still firm and bright green but without that strangely weird squeaky feeling against your teeth a slightly undercooked bean can have.

Courgettes

If you grow courgettes yourself they are a real summer treat, picked fresh from the garden. Courgettes, both green and gold varieties, are lovely sliced and lightly fried in a little oil or butter.

They are also good lightly steamed: three minutes is about right. See **Green Salads** in the **Lighter Lunches and Midweek Suppers** section for raw courgettes.

A Word of Caution about Steamers Steamers are great, but they can boil dry very easily. Bigger, deeper steamers are better than smaller ones since they hold more water and won't need to be topped up for the relatively short time required for steaming vegetables.

Apple Sauce

The quantities here are very elastic; you don't really need exact measurements. The following amount will serve four but you can increase the amount very easily.

Peel, core and slice four or five dessert apples – Cox's are ideal. Add a couple of tablespoons of water, or preferably apple juice, and simmer on the hob until the apples are completely soft. Beat briskly and thoroughly with a wooden spoon until you have a smooth, thick purée.

Useful Note Any leftover apple sauce is perfect on your breakfast cereal (especially muesli) the next morning.

Leftovers

Years ago, people used to make the Sunday joint last through till about Thursday: cold cuts on Monday, stew or shepherd's pie on Tuesday, curry on Wednesday and so on. Anyway, it's still great having leftovers from a roast dinner: you really feel you've got your money's worth! Also, they can be transformed into some of your tastiest, favourite home-cooked meals. All the quantities in this section are approximate.

Delicious Sandwiches, Cold Cuts and Leftover Bits and Pieces

Cold roast meat makes wonderful sandwiches and is great with salads, some pickles or relishes and a baked potato. Alternatively, if you have a few other bits and pieces left over you can serve cold meat with any of the following: stuffing balls, apple sauce, bread sauce or onion sauce, which are all amazingly nice cold. Best of all, you might have some leftover potatoes.

FRIED SLICED POTATOES

If you have some boiled potatoes left over, then you are in for a treat! Slice them into thicknesses of a little less then a centimetre. Heat some oil in a wide, shallow pan and add the potatoes. Turn the heat down to moderate and fry on both sides until golden. Drain on kitchen paper and serve immediately with perhaps a little sprinkling of Maldon Salt.

These are great served with cold meat but equally good with fried eggs and thick slices of ham or as part of a cooked breakfast.

It's worth boiling some potatoes especially to make these. To achieve the proper taste and texture they must be cold when you slice them. Although you can use any kind of potato, new potatoes are particularly good and there is no need to peel them.

Fried Potatoes with Rosemary

If you are feeling a bit fancy and continental then fry the potatoes with a sprinkle of Maldon Salt and some spikes of rosemary, as the Italians do. Cooked this way they are good served with plainly cooked steak or lamb.

FRIED MASHED POTATOES

Mashed potatoes are also great fried. Season them with freshly ground black or white pepper and a little salt. Heat some oil in a pan (not too much) and add the potatoes. Turn the heat down to moderate and fry, turning once or twice until they are cooked through and have a nice golden, crispy crust.

If you have any leftover vegetables such as Brussels sprouts or cabbage, and carrots, you can stir them through the potatoes and fry them all together for a kind of mixed bubble and squeak. Brussels sprouts can be sliced or halved. Alternatively, cook and drain some frozen peas and stir them into the potato before frying: this is fabulous eaten with a little chutney, pickle, or brown sauce.

See also **Tuna Melt** in **Very Quick Light Meals on Toast** for an alternative way of using cold mashed potatoes.

LEFTOVER GRAVY

If you have any gravy left over, cool it quickly and get it into the fridge. Cover it and use within 24 hours. It will add great flavour and thickness to a stew or shepherd's pie the next day. Be sure to heat it thoroughly. Don't reheat it a second time.

SHEPHERD'S PIE

The quantities here assume you only have enough meat left over to serve 2–3. If you have more adjust the quantities accordingly.

Cold roast lamb (or beef) makes a great shepherd's pie: it has more of a nursery texture than shepherd's pie made with mince. Cut the meat into pieces and whiz very briefly in a food processor: the meat should be fairly coarsely minced, not ground into dust. Make up a little gravy by frying **a large onion** in a little **oil** until golden. Sprinkle a **tablespoon of plain flour** into the pan and cook briefly. Stir a **tablespoon of black treacle, a teaspoon of tomato purée** and **a few shakes of Worcestershire sauce** into about **150ml (¼ pint) of hot water** and stir into the pan. Add the minced meat and bring to the boil. Turn the heat down to moderate and simmer for about an hour or until the liquid has thickened and reduced. Add more water, or potato cooking water, if it seems dry, but not too much.

Meanwhile boil about **1 kilo or so (2lb) of potatoes**, drain and mash with **butter** and a little **hot milk, season** to taste.

When the mince is ready, pour into an ovenproof dish (strain off some liquid if it is too sloppy) and spread the mashed potatoes on top. Make lines with a dinner fork across the top and dot with butter so it will brown nicely. Bake in a moderate oven for 20–30 minutes until the top is golden brown.

Serve with peas and crusty bread, and a little tomato ketchup on the side.

MONDAY STEW

This works well with leftover beef or lamb: if you are using lamb, add **25–50g (1–2oz) pearl barley**.

Cut the meat into pieces. Slice **a large onion** and fry in a little **oil** until soft and golden. Peel **a couple of carrots** and slice fairly thinly. Add to the onions and cook briefly. Sprinkle **a tablespoon of plain flour** into the pan and stir for a few moments until it has all mixed in. Stir **2 tablespoons of black treacle, 1 tablespoon of Worcestershire sauce** and **a teaspoon of tomato purée** into about **425ml (¾ pint) of hot water** and add to the pan gradually, stirring throughout. Add your **meat,** bring to the boil, turn down the heat and simmer for an hour or so, until the gravy is thick and everything is cooked through.

Serve with mashed or baked potatoes.

LEFTOVERS CURRY

You can make a fantastic curry with leftover chicken, turkey, beef, lamb or pork. Slice **a large onion** and fry in **a little oil** until soft and golden. Stir in about **a dessertspoon of curry paste** (Madras works well) or curry powder to taste, and cook for a few minutes. Depending on how much meat you have, add **50–110g (2–4oz) of red lentils** to the pan and stir to coat. Cut your **leftover meat** into pieces and add to the pan. Stir so that the meat is fully coated with the curry mixture. Stir in some **hot water: 425ml (¾ pint)** or so and bring to the boil. Turn to a gentle simmer and cook for about an hour or until it has thickened and the flavours have amalgamated.

You can add a couple of **finely sliced carrots** at the beginning as well if you like. Towards the end of the cooking time you might like to add a handful of **sultanas or frozen peas**.

Serve with rice or baked potatoes.

See also: **Lightly Curried Chicken Supper**
Creamy Chicken and Mushrooms
Chicken and Mushroom Pie
Quick Boston Style Beans to serve with slices of cold pork

Christmas roasts
You might start Christmas with some baked ham and salad on Christmas Eve, roast turkey or beef on Christmas Day and then have a few restful days of cold cuts and leftovers after that.

BAKED HAM

Treat yourself to a large piece of gammon from your local butcher at Christmas. Buy a piece big enough for sandwiches and cold cuts for a few days and bake it with something sweet and something spicy (see below). Tell your butcher you want to do this so he will give you a piece with a large enough area of fat for you to work on. Your butcher can advise you on cooking times: it will usually be something like 25 minutes per half kilo or 1lb.

Bake your ham for the required time, but half an hour before the end of the cooking time, take it out of the oven and allow it to cool slightly.

You are now going to take the skin off, so make sure the area is clear of small children and animals and that you are not wearing your best clothes, as a few splashes of hot fat are extremely likely.

Using two large carving forks or a large fork and a fish slice, put the ham on a large board or work surface. If you have an old clean tea towel you can put underneath this will help.

Using a smallish, sharp, kitchen knife rather than a carving knife (too unwieldy) and a dinner fork, slice the skin off the fat so that all the fat is exposed. Don't cut too deeply or you will cut into the meat itself.

Once you have removed all the skin, score some lines across the fat, criss-crossing to make diamond patterns.

Now you are ready to add whichever coating you prefer.

Suggestions for coatings

Demerara sugar and mustard Mix some English mustard (either ready-made from a jar, or mix some powdered mustard with water) and demerara sugar together: use 2 tablespoons of sugar to a teaspoon of mustard. Spread it as best you can (it will be messy!) over the exposed fat. If you are a fan of cloves, stick a few into the fat as well – try to make a regular pattern.

Marmalade and mustard Mix 2 tablespoons of marmalade (without peel is best) with a teaspoon of English mustard (as above).

Demerara sugar and hoi sin sauce Mix a couple of tablespoons of hoi sin sauce with a couple of tablespoons of demerara sugar: this is *exceptionally* messy but *really, really* delicious!

When you have added your chosen coating, put the ham back into the oven, uncovered, for the remaining half an hour of cooking time, or until the sugar is just tinged slightly brown and melting and the ham is fully cooked.

You might like to have your first serving hot, on Christmas Eve, with salad and pickles and baked potatoes, or wait until Boxing Day and cook it then. After that it will provide quite a few sandwiches and cold cuts for a couple more days or so.

A note on Christmas dinner

Cold turkey is very welcome over the Christmas holiday but it can be quite a dense meat to serve hot, combined with all the traditional accompaniments for Christmas Day itself. It is also quite a stressful meal to cook. You *might* consider a joint of beef instead, which is such a treat as it's a bit pricey to have very often. You could start the gravy the day before and just have it with mashed potatoes and vegetables, including Brussels sprouts which, incidentally, seem to go better with beef than turkey. Add some strong English mustard and horseradish sauce and that's it: you don't even need Yorkshire puddings. So, plenty of room for Christmas pudding which, again, seems to follow beef really well, and you have a lovely stress-free morning with time to relax. Plus, it's so easy to just put the leftovers in the fridge afterwards; no desperate dismembering of the turkey and trying to fit it in the fridge when you are just longing to collapse!

If you do have beef for Christmas Day it's quite nice to roast a large chicken for New Year's Day or the Sunday before Christmas and serve it with the traditional Christmas bread sauce, stuffing, little sausages, bacon rolls and cranberry sauce, and Brussels sprouts.

ROASTING A TURKEY

Again, your butcher can advise you about cooking times but it is generally about 25 minutes per half kilo or 1lb in weight. Time your turkey so that it can come out of the oven half an hour or so before you want to eat. It will need to rest so that the juices can settle and also, unless your oven is enormous, you may need the oven clear for your roast potatoes and stuffing balls and so on.

Preheat oven to 220°C (fan oven) or equivalent.

Remove any giblets and fill the cavity with something to add moisture and flavour such as: a couple of apples or satsumas, lemons or even an onion. Slather the breast and legs with softened butter and a good grinding of black or white pepper. There is no need to actually stuff the turkey: you can cook separate stuffing balls.

Wrap loosely with foil and put into the oven. Set the timer for 20 minutes.

After 20 minutes, turn the heat down to 180°C (fan oven) or equivalent. About every hour or so after that, carefully manoeuvre the turkey out of the oven, shutting the oven door again as soon as possible so you don't lose the temperature, and baste the turkey. About half an hour before the turkey is due to come out of the oven, remove the foil so it can brown nicely. The turkey is cooked when the juices run clear. Test different parts of the turkey, as different parts, such as the top of the thighs, will probably cook at different rates.

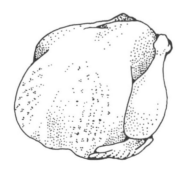

Little sausages and bacon rolls

Cook at 180ºC (fan oven) or equivalent.

If you are having turkey, you can't miss out on dipping the bacon and sausages into the bread sauce! It can be difficult to find really good cocktail sausages so try buying decent chipolatas and dividing them into two. It is really easy to do: just put the chipolata on a board and putting your forefinger in the middle of it, gently roll it backwards and forwards until it starts to separate within the skin. Twist and cut into two. (Incidentally, you can also do this with full-size sausages as well: you end up with two comical looking round fat sausages!)

You can wrap bacon round the sausages if you like, or make separate bacon rolls. Streaky bacon works well, but you can use back bacon if you prefer. Cut the rind off first; kitchen scissors are ideal for this. Stretch each rasher slightly with the back of a knife and cut into two. Roll up each piece and secure with a cocktail stick. You can cook the sausages and the bacon rolls in the same very lightly oiled dish. Cook for about 20–25 minutes, turning after 10 minutes or so.

See the beginning of this section, for **Proper Home-Made Gravy**, **Bread Sauce** and **Home-Made Sage and Onion Stuffing Balls**. With everything else going on it's best to start your gravy the day before and not worry about adding any meat juices; turkey is not noted for its flavoursome gravy juices in any case. Don't forget the **cranberry sauce**!

Dealing with the turkey afterwards

Cool the turkey as quickly as possible afterwards and get it into the fridge. If you think you won't use the legs (great for curries) for a couple of days, put them in the freezer now. On no account leave the turkey hanging around in a warm room all afternoon.

Cleaning roasting dishes

If you are afflicted with sticky burnt pans after the big lunch, try this: fill them with water, warm or hot, and leave a dishwasher tablet in to dissolve. If you happen to be around when the tablet is half dissolved, use it to scrub at the worst bits. This works so well, it's worth keeping a small box of dishwasher tablets to hand, even if you don't have a dishwasher!

GREAT CHRISTMAS SANDWICHES

Here are a few suggestions for turkey and ham:

• Lightly buttered bread, slices of turkey, light sprinkling of salt, mango chutney;

• Lightly buttered bread, slices of cold turkey, slices of cold stuffing, touch of cold bread sauce, pickle or chutney;

• Lightly buttered bread, slices of ham, English mustard, lettuce;

• Bread spread lightly with mayonnaise, slices of turkey, cold ham, lettuce or salad leaves;

• Bread spread lightly with mayonnaise, slices of ham, lettuce or salad leaves, thin slices of cucumber, touch of chutney.

PUDDINGS

Apart from possibly the Sunday roast itself, puddings seem to evoke the strongest culinary memories and loyalties and generate the most deeply cherished routines (What do you mean, there's no apple crumble? But it's Sunday!).

You might not have a proper pudding every day – usually, perhaps, some fruit and yoghurt and maybe occasionally a bit of cake – but it's good to push the boat out once or twice a week and when visitors come round. See also **Cakes** and **Pastry** sections, for more puddingy type recipes.

APPLE CRUMBLE

This recipe uses dessert apples which are firmer and don't need extra sugar rather than the traditional Bramleys which cook to a soft fluff. (It's nice to use Bramleys sometimes, particularly when the new season starts.)

SERVES 4–6

5 or 6 eating apples: Cox's are ideal (if you are using a couple of Bramleys instead, don't forget to add a couple of level tablespoons of sugar, or to taste)

A splash of apple juice or, failing that, water

225g (8oz) plain flour

I teaspoon baking powder

75g (3oz) butter, softened

75g (3oz) sugar

Preheat oven to 180ºC (fan oven) or equivalent.

Peel, core and slice the apples. Cook them gently for a few moments in a splash of apple juice or water until the juices are starting to run and they are softening slightly. Strain off any surplus juice and put the apples into a baking dish.

Sieve the flour and baking powder into a roomy bowl and rub in the butter. Stir in the sugar. Cover the prepared apples with a good couple of centimetres of crumble. Bake for 20–30 minutes until the crumble is pale golden.

Serve with custard, cream or vanilla ice cream. It's also great cold.

Variations
Crumble is such a classic mix and such a treat it's almost a shame to add anything different to it such as oats or ground almonds. You could sometimes swap an ounce or two of plain flour for spelt flour or kamut flour though, as they both have a lovely sweetish edge to them.

BREAD AND BUTTER PUDDING

This is another well-established favourite. It might give the impression of being a bit rough and ready but actually it needs quite delicate handling in a moderate oven if the egg custard part is to turn out right. Sandwich the dried fruit in between the layers of bread and butter rather than having any scattered on top, otherwise the finished pudding could be strewn with a few little black cinders!

You will need a greased 3-pint capacity ovenproof dish

Preheat oven to 160ºC (fan oven) or equivalent.

Cut the crusts off the bread (or leave them on if you prefer) and spread the slices with butter. Cut them into triangles or squares and arrange a layer across the bottom of the dish. Scatter the dried fruit over the bread. Arrange the rest of the bread across the top.

Beat the egg yolks and milk lightly together and stir in the sugar and vanilla. Pour over the buttered bread and fruit and leave to stand for half an hour or so.

You must allow the custard to soak into the bread or the texture of the pudding won't be right and any loose custard will be in danger of curdling in the heat of the oven: the finished pudding should be soft and mellow on the bottom and lightly crisp on top.

Bake for approximately 30 minutes until the top is crisp and golden and the bottom has set.

Variations
You might like to enrich the custard by reducing the milk by a couple of tablespoons and making up the quantity with a couple of spoonfuls of cream. You could use slices of brioche or panettone instead of bread and include a little finely chopped dried apricot in the dried fruit or add a little finely chopped candied peel. Something else you might like to try is to spread the buttered bread with a little marmalade as well.

SERVES 4–6

4–5 slices of white bread, preferably a day or two old
Butter for spreading
50g (2oz) mixed dried fruit: raisins, sultanas, currants
2 egg yolks
275ml (½ pint) milk
25g (1oz) unrefined caster sugar
¼ teaspoon vanilla extract or vanilla bean paste

Banana Custard

This is not so much a recipe as a serving suggestion.

SERVES 4

Make up a pint of custard using **2 rounded tablespoons of custard powder**, **2 level tablespoons of sugar** and **570ml (1 pint) milk**. Pour into a serving bowl. Slice **two or three bananas** into the custard and stir.

If your family is divided into those who prefer their bananas hot and slightly soggy, and those who like them cool and firm, you may prefer to put the bananas and a jug of custard on the table and let everyone sort themselves out.

Banoffee Pie and Baby Banoffee Pies

*You can make this the authentic way, which involves boiling a can of condensed milk, unopened, for 3 hours. This is scary but it does work and is quite safe – **provided you keep an eye on it, top up the water regularly and let it cool right down before you open the can!** However, the house also usually becomes a bit too steamy. Alternatively, you can empty the condensed milk into a tightly covered ovenproof dish and heat gently in a low oven for about 3 hours. Again, this works, after a fashion, but it's not completely foolproof.*

The safest and easiest option is to use a jar of dulce de leche: ready-made caramelised milk. This recipe gives the option for one large pie or four smaller ones. The large one is more traditional, the smaller ones involve a lot less ooze and mess when slicing!

The large pie could serve 4–6 or even 6–8 if everyone just has a sliver, as it is rather rich.

110g (4oz) digestive biscuits (usually 9 biscuits)
50g (2oz) butter
25g (1oz) unrefined caster sugar
1 jar of dulce de leche (you probably won't need it all)
2–3 bananas
284ml (½ pint) whipping or double cream, whisked to soft peaks, with either an electric whisk or a hand-operated rotary one
A little cocoa powder or grated chocolate to decorate

You will need either a 17cm (7in) loose-bottomed cake tin or four 9cm (3½ in) crumpet or rosti rings and a large board or baking tray

Crush the digestive biscuits: the easiest way is to put them inside a plastic bag and go over them with a rolling pin. Melt the butter and sugar gently in a saucepan over a moderate heat and stir in the biscuit crumbs. Press the biscuit mix into either a 17cm (7in) loose-bottomed cake tin or 4 crumpet rings on a board or baking tray.

Leave to cool and harden. Spread dulce de leche over the biscuit base and then slice a banana or two over the top. Spread the cream over the top. Decorate with grated chocolate or a sprinkling of cocoa powder. This doesn't store very well as the base goes soggy and the bananas go a bit soft and brown. Best to eat it all at once, then!

CHOCOLATE BLANCMANGE WITH CINNAMON

This has a lovely flavour: if you didn't know it had cinnamon in it you might not be able to put your finger on the flavour as the taste is almost citrus-like. If you prefer, you can make it in the microwave.

You will need either a 1 litre (2 pint/quart) Pyrex jug or a heavy-bottomed milk saucepan

Sieve the cornflour, cocoa powder and cinnamon carefully into your jug (microwave) or a bowl (hob). Stir in the sugar. Take 2 tablespoons or so of the milk and mix to a smooth paste with a metal spoon.

Microwave method
Stir the rest of the cold milk in gradually. Once it is all mixed put it into the microwave on High for 2 minutes. Remove and stir well. Repeat. You may have to do this two or three more times and the last time may only take a minute or less: it depends on your microwave. Once you see the mixture looks thick and glossy (it may begin to rise up in the jug slightly) it is ready. Take it out and give it a really good stir with a wooden spoon. Cool slightly and pour it into one big serving dish or several smaller ones.

Hob method
Put the rest of the milk to heat on the hob until it is almost, but not quite, boiling. Pour it onto the cocoa mixture, stirring constantly with a wooden spoon. Wash out the saucepan and pour the mixture back. Return to the hob and cook on a medium heat, stirring all the time, until the mixture is thick and glossy. Cool slightly and pour into serving dishes, as before. Leave to set in a cool place or refrigerate.

This is lovely on its own or with any kind of cream: a spoonful of whipped or clotted cream is especially nice.

SERVES 4–6

50g (2oz) cornflour
50g (2oz) cocoa powder
1 teaspoon ground
   cinnamon
110g (4oz) unrefined
   caster sugar
570ml (1 pint) milk

HOME-MADE VANILLA ICE CREAM

Although you can make this without an ice cream machine, it is much easier with one. The sort of machine where you put the bowl into the freezer is fairly inexpensive – less than the cost of a pair of children's shoes – and it's useful to have one. This is known as custard-based ice cream, because you make an egg custard to start with. It's the vanilla that really makes this ice cream, so try to get something good quality and avoid 'vanilla flavouring'. Vanilla bean paste is great for this as it has the tiny black seeds in it that look most professional speckled through the ice cream. If you don't like the seeds, go for the extract instead. Alternatively, a vanilla pod will give the best flavour of all.

MAKES about a litre

6 very fresh egg yolks
¼ teaspoon of vanilla bean paste or vanilla extract (not vanilla flavouring)
75g (3 oz) unrefined caster sugar
275ml (½ pint) milk (semi-skimmed is fine)
275ml (½ pint) double cream

Put the egg yolks into a roomy bowl with the vanilla and sugar. Separate the eggs using two dessertspoons or an egg separator, rather than passing them between the two halves of the shell, as the mixture is only going to be cooked very lightly.

Beat the egg yolks and sugar together. Warm the milk in a smallish heavy-bottomed saucepan until it is almost, but not quite, boiling. Pour it into the egg mixture, beating gently all the time.

Wash out the saucepan and put the mixture back. Return to the heat and cook gently, stirring all the time until the mixture coats the spoon very lightly; you might notice a very slight deepening of colour when it's ready. Take it off the heat immediately and pour into a Pyrex measuring jug. If you leave it in the metal pan it will carry on cooking slightly and may start to scramble and curdle. (If the mixture does curdle a bit, pour it discreetly through a sieve.) Leave to cool and stir in the cream.

The next stage is much easier if you have an ice cream machine. If you do, follow the maker's instructions from this stage.

If you don't, stir the mixture thoroughly, or better still whisk it, and pour it into a lidded plastic freezer box and put it into the freezer. After an hour or so, take it out of the freezer and stir it through, beating it quite vigorously with a wooden spoon: this is to break up any large ice crystals that will be forming. Return to the freezer. Repeat after another 30 minutes to an hour, and then again after another 30 minutes to an hour. The finished ice cream will have a slightly rougher texture than the machine-made one, which will make it seem even more authentically home-made!

It's best to eat home-made ice cream within a couple of days of making if you can as it does tend to get very hard when it has been in the freezer for a while. Take it out of the freezer for 20 minutes or so before you want to serve it.

LEMON POSSET

This is a simplified version of a really old recipe. Originally possets were more of an alcoholic eggnog than a pudding. This is just a shadow of its former self, but it's lovely and light: it's very easy to make and has only three ingredients.

Put the cream and sugar into a heavy-bottomed pan and bring to the boil, stirring constantly. Once it is boiling, keep it going for a couple of minutes, still stirring. Remove from the heat, add the lemon juice and stir it well in. Cool slightly and pour into individual serving dishes or ramekins. Leave in a cool place. The acid in the lemon juice will react with the milk and it will set beautifully. Eat the same day. If you have any left over, it will still be nice to eat the next day but the lemon juice will start to separate out again.

Although this pudding is all cream, it works well with a tiny bit more cream on the side or poured over the top. Obviously, you won't be eating this every day!

SERVES 4

570ml (1 pint) double
  cream
150g (5oz) unrefined
  caster sugar
Juice of 2 lemons

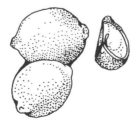

OLD-FASHIONED RICE PUDDING

Puddings don't have to be all glitz and glamour! Sometimes it's nice to have something a bit plain and soothing. This is nothing like the rice pudding that comes in a tin. The grains of rice are much smaller and the pudding is very white in colour, not that deep, almost pinkish-cream shade of the tinned version. If you like, you can replace some of the milk with cream to make it creamier but, in a sense, that defeats the object; this is meant to be quite plain. The only awkward part is that it takes a couple of hours to cook, and it needs to be cooked in a low oven, which is difficult if you want to cook the first course at a higher temperature at the same time. If your oven is not a fan oven, you could try placing the pudding on the very bottom shelf.

SERVES 4–6

110g (4 oz) pudding rice
2 rounded tablespoons –
 about 40g (1½ oz) –
 unrefined granulated
 sugar
Just over 425 ml (¾ pint)
 milk, full cream if
 possible (gold top would
 be best of all)
Knob of butter and
 nutmeg to finish

Soak the rice in water overnight.

Preheat oven to 150ºC (fan oven) or equivalent.

Drain the rice and put it into an ovenproof dish with the sugar and milk. Leave for at least half an hour. When it is time to put it into the oven, put a knob of butter on top and grate quite a lot of nutmeg over it. Bake for an hour or two, or until the rice is completely soft and the top of the pudding is nicely browned.

Serve warm, but it is also nice cold. Having said that cream is unnecessary, actually, once the pudding is cold, it is lovely with a little cream poured over the top!

✓ **Useful Note** A bare 425ml (¾ pint) of milk will give you a pudding where virtually all of the milk is absorbed and 570ml (1 pint) will give you a very milky pudding. Try to aim somewhere between the two.

SEMOLINA PUDDING

This is another plain and soothing pudding. It is surprisingly nutritious and can be useful if someone is recovering from an illness, providing they can digest wheat and milk: use whole milk if they need building up. You don't have to use vanilla but it is a nice addition.

Put the semolina into a heavy-bottomed milk pan and stir in the milk gradually. Bring it to boil on the hob, stirring constantly, turn down the heat and let it bubble gently for a moment or two, stirring all the time. Remove from the heat and stir in the sugar and vanilla.

You can bake this in the oven if you like (pour into a baking dish, dot it with a little butter and bake in a preheated oven at 160ºC (fan oven) or equivalent for about 30 minutes or until golden on top) but it is equally nice served straight from the saucepan. You might like to try it with some stewed fruit: summer berries go especially well.

SERVES 4

50g (2oz) semolina
570ml (1 pint) semi-
    skimmed milk
1 slightly rounded
    tablespoon unrefined
    caster sugar (don't make
    it too sweet)
¼ teaspoon good-quality
    vanilla extract or vanilla
    bean paste

STEWED FRUIT

You never seem to hear of stewed fruit these days: we had it frequently when I was a child, particularly at my grandma's house. Her willow pattern dishes with a flat rim were very handy for putting the stones on if it was plums. Grandma used to count the stones using a rhyme that apparently foretold who you were going to marry: tinker, tailor, soldier, sailor, rich man, poor man, beggar man, thief. Obviously, the choice was a bit limited! Anyway, stewed fruit, which isn't so much stewed as gently cooked, tastes great and is quick and easy. Try serving it warm with custard or Greek yoghurt or cold on your breakfast cereal.

You can stew most kinds of fruit: apples, pears, plums, rhubarb, gooseberries or summer berries. Only add a small amount of water (or apple juice works well), cook over a moderate heat, and add sugar to taste if necessary: caster sugar (preferably unrefined) is best as it dissolves quickly but you can use granulated.

Apples: peel, core, slice and add a splash of water or apple juice. Cook, stirring gently, from time to time, until tender. If you are using Bramleys you will probably need about a tablespoon of sugar to every 450g (1lb).

Pears: stewing is useful if you have a glut of pears; they are great on cereal. Peel, core, quarter and cook as above; you may need a little sugar.

Plums: leave them whole; if you try to remove the stones when they are raw you can end up with a plum massacre, and the flavour is better with them in. Add a little water and sugar to taste. Fantastic served with thick cream with a little Amaretto liqueur stirred through.

Rhubarb: trim and remove any loose ribbons of skin. Cut into short lengths. You will need quite a bit of sugar, probably 75–100g (3–4oz) to every 700g (1½lb). Add very little water.

Gooseberries: top and tail and add sugar to taste: about 75–100g (3–4oz) to every 450g (lb). Cook gently in 1–2 tablespoons of water. You might prefer to sieve out the skins and seeds and have a gooseberry purée instead. (See **Gooseberry Fool** on page 113.) This is lovely on breakfast cereal, vanilla ice cream, or with a dollop of Greek yoghurt.

Summer berries: berries such as red, white and blackcurrants, raspberries, blueberries, blackberries work well as a mixture. This is useful if you have a few oddments of different fruit. You can add a few strawberries for variety although it seems almost a shame to cook them! A few cherries also work well. When you are washing berries, lower them gently into a bowl of water rather than washing them in a colander under the tap: this bruises them and you lose precious juice. Lift them gently out of the water into a colander to drain and cook them in the water that clings to them. Add sugar to taste if necessary. These are great warm or cold with a dollop of Greek yoghurt, with ice cream, or as a filling for pancakes.

Quick and easy topping and tailing of frozen currants

If you find yourself with enough red, white or blackcurrants to freeze try this simple method. Wash and dry the currants and freeze them, as they are, in a freezer bag or box. When you are ready to use them, tip them, still frozen, into a bowl of water. Most of the debris will come off and float on top of the water and you can skim it off.

GOOSEBERRY FOOL

This beautiful summer treat is probably made on only a handful of precious occasions every year during the gooseberry season. The old-fashioned green gooseberries generally make the best-flavoured fools. Serve in small helpings as it's rather rich.

Wash the gooseberries and dry them thoroughly: if you don't, once you start to top and tail, the tops you have taken off will stick to the rest annoyingly! Also, if you wash the fruit afterwards, some of the ones you have inadvertently cut into will start to break up before you get them into the pan.

Topping and tailing gooseberries looks as though it will be a bit of a fiddle but it only takes a minute or two to top and tail 450g.

Work with a fairly sharp short-handled knife (a long handle is awkward) and work over a container to put the bits in, with the unprepared gooseberries on one side and the saucepan of prepared ones on the other.

Add the sugar and water and simmer the gooseberries for 20–30 minutes until tender. Strain off the juice and leave to cool. You need to remove the skins and seeds next: push them through a sieve with a wooden spoon. Put the sieved purée in the fridge to chill.

Whip the cream with an electric whisk or a hand-operated rotary whisk until it forms soft peaks. Fold the gooseberry purée into the cream and serve in individual glass dishes. If you are entertaining, a biscuit on the side is always appreciated. See **Lemon Biscuits** (page 204) and **Shrewsbury Type Biscuits** (page 206).

SERVES 4–6

450g (1lb) gooseberries
75–110g (3–4oz) unrefined
    caster sugar
1–2 tablespoons water
275ml (½ pint) double
    cream

Quick and easy topping and tailing of frozen gooseberries

If you find yourself with enough gooseberries to freeze try this simple method. Wash and dry the gooseberries and freeze them, as they are, in a freezer bag or box. When you are ready to use them, tip them, still frozen, onto a clean, dry tea towel. Work with no more than 225g (½lb) at a time. Wrap the tea towel round the gooseberries and rub them vigorously through the cloth. Most of the tops and stalks will come off. Remove the rest by picking up each gooseberry in one hand and rubbing the top and tail off with the tea towel in the other. The job is done in no time.

GOOSEBERRY AND ELDERFLOWER FOOL

This is exactly the same as above, but stir a teaspoon (or to personal taste) of undiluted elderflower cordial through the gooseberry purée before you fold in the cream.

GOOSEBERRY FOOL ICE CREAM

Either of these Gooseberry Fools make the most delicious ice cream: it's a touch on the tart and sophisticated side and more popular with adults than children. Serve with a biscuit on the side: **Lemon Biscuits, Orange Biscuits** *and* **Shrewsbury Type Biscuits** *(pages 203–206) all go well.*

SERVES 4–6

275ml (½ pint) sieved stewed gooseberries, including juice, made with 450g (1lb) gooseberries and 75–110g (3–4oz) sugar (see above)
275ml (½ pint) double cream, whipped to soft peaks

You will need to include the juice for this recipe. Make the gooseberry purée as in the previous recipe but make up to 275ml (½ pint) with some (or all) of the strained juice.

Fold the cream and purée together and finish in an ice cream machine. See **Home-Made Vanilla Ice Cream** (page 108) for more details.

RHUBARB AND CUSTARD FOOL

*For some reason, gooseberry fools always seem sophisticated – a light whisper of a pudding – while rhubarb fools seem a bit more homely and less rich. This is a very homely version made with custard and cream: it retains more fruit texture than the **Gooseberry Fool**, which is completely smooth. Main crop rhubarb works well in this recipe but the new season's pink rhubarb is best of all.*

Wash the rhubarb, remove any long ribbons of outer skin and cut into chunks. Cook gently with the sugar and the barest amount of water until soft but still in distinct pieces. Strain and leave to cool.

Put the custard powder in a bowl with a little of the milk and mix to a smooth paste (there is no need to add sugar as there is enough in the rhubarb). Put the rest of the milk in a saucepan and heat almost to boiling point. Stir the hot milk briskly into the custard paste. Wash the milk pan and return the custard to it. Bring it to the boil over a moderate heat, stirring constantly.

Cool the custard slightly. Beat the strained rhubarb with a wooden spoon until you have a rough purée. Stir in the cooling custard, mixing it all together thoroughly. Put it in the fridge to chill.

Once the rhubarb and custard are completely cold, whip the cream to soft peaks with an electric whisk or a hand-held rotary whisk. Fold the cream into the rhubarb and custard and spoon into a serving bowl or bowls.

SERVES 4–6

450g (1lb) rhubarb
75g (3oz) unrefined
  granulated sugar
1–2 tablespoons water
1 rounded tablespoon
  custard powder
150ml (¼ pint) milk
150ml (¼ pint) cream

RHUBARB AND CUSTARD FOOL ICE CREAM

Rhubarb and Custard Fool, just like **Gooseberry Fool**, makes *the* most delicious ice cream, possibly even more so. An **Orange Biscuit** (see page 203) on the side goes very nicely.

Prepare everything as for the previous recipe. Retain the strained juice and add 150ml (¼ pint) of it to the fool mixture, stirring thoroughly.

Finish in an ice cream machine and transfer to a lidded plastic box. See **Home-Made Vanilla Ice Cream** (page 108) for more details.

PANCAKES

Serve these with lemon and sugar, runny honey or maple syrup, a squeeze of orange, blackcurrant or cherry jam or whatever you fancy.

SERVES 4–6

For the basic pancake recipe
110g (4oz) plain flour
1 egg
300ml (½ pint) semi-skimmed milk
Pinch of salt
Butter and/or oil (melted butter gives the best flavour)

Sieve the flour into a bowl large enough to give you room to manoeuvre, and make a well in the middle. Tip the egg into the well and stir it in, then gradually add the milk, stirring as you go, until you have a batter the consistency of thin cream. Stir in the salt. Use a large dinner fork to stir everything together and then give it a good whisk with a coiled-spring whisk. Leave it to stand for about 10 minutes at room temperature and stir it again just before using. Pour the batter into a jug, for ease of use.

Brush an 18cm (7in) non-stick frying pan with melted butter, or oil if you prefer. Put the pan on to heat, on a medium to high setting, and get it really hot. Pour the batter into the middle of the pan, from quite a height, until you have covered an area about the size of a large fried egg. Then, flick the pan in a circular motion until the batter spreads to cover nearly the whole of the pan. Cook the pancake for a couple of minutes until it turns from translucent to opaque, and when you shake the pan the pancake makes a kind of scratchy, shushing sound. Flip it over with a fish slice and cook for another couple of minutes, again until you can shake the pan as before. Flip it over again for a final check. Brush the fish slice with butter or oil if it won't go under the pancake easily.

The pan should be completely dry with no trace of butter or oil after each pancake: try brushing the pan with melted butter between each one but do bear in mind, if you are going to do this, the pan will be very hot so the brush must be made from actual bristle and not nylon!

Incidentally, if you find yourself having to provide batter for a pancake party, a large plastic milk container is ideal to carry it in. If you have only just finished using it, you don't even have to wash it out!

FRESH ORANGE JELLY

This is lovely and refreshing and great for children or as one of several puddings for a posh grown-up dinner.

Pour the hot water into a measuring jug and sprinkle the gelatine over the top. Stir briskly with a dinner fork. Once the gelatine is dissolved make up to 570 ml (1 pint) with the orange juice. Taste and add sugar as needed. Stir in the orange flower water if using. Pour into a serving dish or dishes, cover and leave in a cool place to set.

SERVES 4–6
MAKES 570 ml (1 pint)

150 ml (¼ pint) hot water
2 sachets powdered gelatine
425ml (¾ pint) juice
   squeezed from 3–4
   oranges
1 level dessertspoon
   unrefined caster sugar,
   or to taste
Few drops orange flower
   water (optional)

Orange Jelly Cups and Smiley Orange Teeth

These are nice to do for parties – the cups for grown-up events and the teeth for children's – although it is quite hard going scooping out the oranges. Keep back some of the squeezed orange halves from making the jelly (or all of them if you feel up to it) and scrape away all that's left of the orange flesh using a teaspoon. You may be able to pull some of the membrane away with your fingers. Try not to make a hole in the peel, particularly when removing the central pith.

Once you have several clean halves, stand them on some crumpled foil laid on top of a baking tray to keep them upright. Pour the jelly into the orange halves and leave to set.

If these are for adults arrange them on individual plates or in little dishes. If they are for children, once they are *completely* set, cut each half into two or three segments using a very sharp knife. The idea is that each child can then suck the jelly out of each segment and use the empty peel to make a big scary grin. Great for Hallowe'en!

Orange Juice Jelly

If you don't actually have any oranges to hand you can make the jelly with orange juice from a carton: freshly squeezed or from concentrate. If you use juice from concentrate the jelly will be cloudy rather than clear but it still looks nice and tastes good.

Orange Jelly with Mandarin Oranges

Another variation is to use a tin of mandarin orange segments in natural juice. Strain the juice from the fruit and use to make the jelly, topped up with fresh orange juice or from a carton. Put the orange segments into the serving dish(es) and pour the jelly over the top.

CRANBERRY DESSERT JELLY

This is a lovely jelly to make around Christmas time for a light pudding: it is refreshing and has a beautiful jewel-like colour. If you make both cranberry and orange individual jellies they work really well served side by side together to give people a choice. A little dollop of thick cream, or some Greek yoghurt with a little caster sugar and vanilla extract or vanilla bean paste stirred through it, are a great accompaniment. Cranberries on their own are so sour and drying they make your mouth feel furry and puckered immediately, so you will have to buy sweetened cranberry juice or cranberry juice drink. Look for a good-quality one sweetened with actual sugar rather than anything artificial, and with as few additives as possible: the quality and flavour of the finished jelly will depend entirely on the quality of the juice.

SERVES 4–6

150ml (¼ pint) hot water
2 sachets powdered
    gelatine
150ml (¼ pint) cranberry
    juice drink (see above)

Measure the hot water into a measuring jug and sprinkle the gelatine over the top. Stir briskly with a dinner fork until the gelatine has melted. Pour in the cranberry juice and stir. Pour into the serving dish or dishes, cover, and leave to set in a cool place.

TRIFLES

Trifles are a huge favourite with a lot of people: somehow they seem to bring back childhood memories yet feel a bit sophisticated at the same time. Trifles are usually for fairly special occasions so you could bake a sponge especially for the bottom layer but bought sponge fingers work well. A home-made egg custard would give a touch of luxury but custard made with custard powder is good too. You will need a special glass serving dish to arrange it all in.

CLASSIC TRIFLE

Spread the sponge fingers with the jam and arrange in the dish. Pour the sherry over them and allow it to soak in. Make up the custard, cool slightly and pour carefully over the sponge. Cover and leave in a cool place to set. Once the custard is completely cold, and not too far ahead of when you want to serve it, whip the cream using an electric whisk or a hand-held rotary whisk and spread over the top. Decorate.

SERVES 6

Enough sponge fingers to
    cover the bottom of
    your serving dish
Raspberry jam for
    spreading, either
    seedless or pushed
    through a sieve
A splash or two of sherry
    (optional)
570ml (1 pint) of custard
    made with 2 generous
    tablespoons of custard
    powder and 2 level
    tablespoons of sugar
Enough whipped double
    or whipping cream to
    cover
Flaked almonds to
    decorate (or a
    decoration of your
    choice)

Orange Trifle

SERVES 6

Enough ratafia biscuits (or
 sponge fingers, if
 preferred) to cover the
 bottom of your serving
 dish
Splash or two of orange
 liqueur (optional)
1 pint of fresh orange jelly,
 as above (or orange jelly
 with mandarin oranges
 works well)
570ml (1 pint) of custard,
 as above
Enough whipped double
 or whipping cream to
 cover
More ratafias (or flaked
 almonds) to decorate
 (or a decoration of your
 choice)

Arrange the sponge fingers in your serving dish. Pour the liqueur over them and allow it to soak in. Make up the jelly and allow it to cool slightly. Pour it carefully over the sponge. Cover and leave in a cool place to set. Once the jelly has set completely, make the custard and allow it to cool as much as possible before pouring carefully over the jelly. Cover and leave in a cool place. Whip the cream, spread over the trifle and decorate.

If you prefer, you can make the trifles in individual dishes.

Decorations
Good trifle decorations include: flaked almonds, blanched almonds, ratafias, crystallised violets and rose petals, pastel sugared almonds and gold and silver sugared almonds, and hundreds and thousands for children.

CHRISTMAS PUDDING

*Christmas pudding is extremely easy to make – you just literally assemble your ingredients and stir them all together – and it can be quite a fun thing (although a bit messy, obviously) to do with the whole family. The main point of making your own, though, is that it is so **delicious**! This is a comparatively light and fruity pudding, just right for after the Christmas meal. If you would like something a fraction more substantial, add 25–50g (1–2oz) of fresh breadcrumbs with the rest of the ingredients. As with any Christmas Pudding, this has excellent keeping qualities.*

During preparation, try to avoid any long shreds of carrot: you may like to finely chop the carrot after grating as well. Similarly, try to avoid any long shreds of lemon or orange zest: use a lemon zester in a brisk up and down movement.

Mix everything together, except the flour, juices, stout and brandy, and then sieve in the flour and stir in the liquids. At this stage everybody can join in with the stirring and make wishes, pose for photos and what have you. Cover and leave everything in a cool place overnight for the flavours to mingle and develop.

To cook the pudding

You can steam this pudding in the usual way – it takes about 2 hours – but it's much easier to microwave it. It is much quicker, the result is just as good and you don't have to put up with a houseful of steam. The microwaving is very straightforward but you must do it in stages and keep to the resting times; bear in mind it is quite a combustible mixture. Also, **don't miscount and overcook it** or you will dry it out too much.

Grease your basin(s) and pour in your pudding mixture, stopping a couple of centimetres or so (about an inch) below the rim. Cover with greaseproof paper and tie with string.

MAKES one 1¼ litre (2 pint) pudding or two 570 ml (1 pint) ones

½ teaspoon each: mixed spice, grated nutmeg, ground cinnamon, ground coriander, ground ginger
50g (2oz) shredded suet
110g (4oz) each: currants, raisins, sultanas
25g (1oz) candied peel (not mixed peel), fairly finely sliced and cut into small pieces
1 eating apple, peeled and grated
1 carrot, peeled and finely grated (try to avoid any long shreds)
2 tablespoons black treacle
50g (2oz) plain flour
Finely grated zest and juice of ½ lemon and ½ orange
65 ml (2½fl oz) stout
1 tablespoon brandy

For a 1¼ litre (2 pint) pudding

Cook on full power for 2 minutes and rest for 1 minute. Repeat until the pudding has had 10 minutes' cooking time in total.

For a 570 ml (1 pint) pudding

Cook on full power for 5 minutes in total, following the instructions above.

For 275 ml (½ pint) and 150 ml (¼ pint) puddings

Cook on full power for 3 minutes in total, stopping and resting halfway through.

Leave to stand for 10 minutes before turning out, leave to cool and then wrap in clean greaseproof paper and foil and store in a cool place until Christmas.

To freeze the pudding

If you are making extra they will freeze perfectly. Wrap in greaseproof paper and foil and then in a securely tied freezer bag.

To reheat the pudding on Christmas Day

To reheat, remove the pudding from its wrapping and return it to a greased basin, cover with clean greaseproof paper and tie with string.

Cook 570 ml (1 pint) and 1¼ litre (2 pint) puddings on full power for 5 minutes. Rest halfway through, as above.

Cook 275 ml (½ pint) and 150 ml (¼ pint) puddings on full power for 3 minutes, rest halfway through.

Leave to stand for 2 minutes before turning out.

This pudding is lovely served with any of the usual accompaniments but it is *especially good* served with clotted cream.

Very Quick Light Meals on Toast

A note about toast

Nearly everyone loves toast. Even the smell of it is cosy and reassuring. It's hard to imagine breakfasts without toast, or a toastless winter teatime, or not being able to have toast for a quick lunch.

It is very simple to make perfect toast but it can be easy to spoil it. It's essential to have decent bread, preferably from an uncut loaf that you slice yourself. It doesn't really matter whether it is brown or white or wholegrain; all make good toast. Also, butter is usually better for flavour than spreads and margarines. Finally, burnt toast is horrible: toast should be a lovely golden brown, and it should rest for a few seconds to let the steam escape and stop it from going bendy and soggy. You can leave it in the toaster for a few moments or prop it up against something.

The following recipes or serving suggestions are all based around toast and are very easy, but substantial enough to keep you going.

WELSH RAREBIT

Welsh Rarebit makes a lovely lunch, but it is just as good at teatime cut into triangles or as a light supper. Serve it with some leafy salad and sliced tomatoes. Coleslaw also goes surprisingly well. Welsh Rarebit is quite often served in teashops and it is interesting to compare the different recipes and methods. Some versions contain beer or stout, some contain flour, some are very hot and spicy, and some are a bit mellower. This one is just about right.

SERVES 1–2 but it's easy
   to double or treble
   quantities

50g (2oz) mature Cheddar,
   grated
1 medium egg yolk
2 tablespoons semi-
   skimmed milk
Pinch of dry mustard or
   dab of English ready-
   made mustard from a
   jar
Few shakes of
   Worcestershire sauce
2 slices of decent bread,
   brown or white, not too
   thickly cut
Butter for spreading

Combine the cheese, egg yolk, milk, mustard and Worcestershire sauce in a small heavy saucepan and cook on a medium heat, stirring pretty much all the time. It will thin down and then thicken slightly again as it amalgamates and starts to bubble gently. Don't take your eye off it or have the heat too high or the egg will split and scramble.

Once the cheese has melted and the mixture is smooth, take it off the heat and set aside; it will thicken even more. Lightly toast the bread and allow it to cool slightly before buttering: this is because the toast needs to be crisp to support the rarebit. Spread the cheese mixture onto the toast and grill until bubbling and golden.

You might like to try adding wholegrain mustard for a change: the flavour is good and the mustard seeds speckled through the rarebit look attractive.

LIGHT AND LUSCIOUS VERSION

This is possibly even more delicious than the original: instead of 2 tablespoons of milk, use **a generous heaped tablespoon** of **half fat crème fraiche**.

BLUE CHEESE VERSION

You can make Welsh Rarebit with blue cheese as well. It's particularly good just after Christmas if you have some Stilton or similar left over. Use **blue cheese** instead of the Cheddar. Be careful not to over-brown it under the grill though or the flavour will be ruined. Lovely with some **cranberry sauce** on the side, some **green salad** and **a few walnuts**.

VERY WELSH VERSION

This is an extra topping for either of the Cheddar recipes above. Peel and slice **a small leek per person** and soften in **a little butter**. Spread most of the prepared rarebit over the toast, lift the leeks from the pan, drain briefly on kitchen paper and put on the top of the rarebit. Finish off with the rest of the rarebit and put under the grill.

Quantities given for the following recipes are per person unless otherwise specified.

TOASTED CHEESE

Toasted cheese is a real favourite with most people. Make sure the toast has cooled and crisped slightly before you put the cheese on top. Some people butter it first, some don't. Whether or not you butter the whole slice, it's nice to butter the edges of the toast so they crisp up nicely under the grill. A generous layer of grated cheese melts more evenly and satisfyingly than sliced, and it also goes further.

Crumbly cheeses such as Cheshire, Wensleydale, Caerphilly and Lancashire all toast brilliantly and make a change from Cheddar. Alternatively, 'stringy' or 'rubbery' cheeses like Edam or Gouda toast well. Small triangles of toasted cheese, dusted with a little cayenne or paprika pepper, are great with a bowl of soup.

CHEESY CHILLI CRUMPETS

The chilli makes this into quite a bracing lunch or teatime snack. Toast the **crumpets** and **butter** lightly. Arrange some **grated cheese** carefully on top and add a **thin slice or two of red chilli**. Put under a hot grill until golden and bubbling and the chilli is very slightly charred.

CHEESE BEANO

This is perfect for a toasty children's tea.

A small serving of baked beans 2 eggs 2 slices of decent bread, brown or white Butter for spreading Thinly sliced or grated Cheddar	Heat the beans, poach the eggs, and lightly toast the bread. Cool the toast slightly, butter it and spoon the beans on top. Cover with the cheese and put under the grill until the cheese is bubbling. To serve: top with the eggs and arrange any leftover beans around the side.

REALLY QUICK GARLIC BREAD

This is very quick and easy.

Lightly toast the bread. Meanwhile, mix enough softened butter with the garlic. Allow the toast to cool slightly and spread with the garlic butter. Cut each slice into two diagonally and serve immediately.

Quantities to suit of:

Fairly thickly sliced decent bread (white is more traditional for garlic bread)
Softened butter for spreading
Finely sliced garlic clove or a little minced garlic from a jar

TOASTY PIZZA

This is a great quick snack and popular with children.

Lightly toast the bread and spread with the garlic butter. Spread the tomato sauce on top (not too thickly) and add some cheese. Add your other chosen ingredients. Put under a hot grill until the cheese is bubbling. Cut in half diagonally and serve immediately.

Quantities to suit of:

Decent bread, sliced fairly thickly, brown or white
Garlic butter (as above)
Easy Tomato Sauce for Pasta (see page 71), or from a jar
Grated Cheddar cheese
Anything else you fancy: a bit of ham, some olives, an anchovy or two, some jalapeno peppers, some lightly fried sliced mushrooms, a grinding of black pepper, a sprinkle of oregano (oregano has a really appetising pizza aroma as it heats up)

TOASTY PIZZA: CHUNKY STYLE

Slice chunks from a **French stick**, split in half, toast lightly under the grill and proceed as above.

TOASTY PIZZA: EXTRA SPECIAL VERSION

This looks impressive for parties. Slice a **baguette**, not too thickly, butter and spread with tomato sauce, as before, and top with slices of **mozzarella**. Stick to just one extra ingredient such as one **black olive** per slice. A single **basil** leaf works well too but put it on after grilling.

TARAMASALATA ON TOAST

This is not a recipe as such, just a suggestion! Obviously, you would normally eat taramasalata with pitta bread but just sometimes it is nice to have it on toast. Toast your bread lightly, allow it to cool and crisp slightly and butter very sparingly, then spread with **taramasalata**.

ANCHOVY TOAST

*This may not look like the most tantalising thing you could ever spread on your toast but it tastes absolutely delicious. Use actual butter for the toast as you need the sweet creaminess of the butter to balance the saltiness of the anchovies. Toast made from the **Easy Potato Loaf** in the Bread section is exceptionally good with this. The quantities given are for a very small amount but, unless you have a houseful, you won't need very much as it's rather powerful.*

50g tin of anchovies in oil	Whiz the anchovies, including their oil, and the lemon juice, cayenne and black pepper together in the food processor, or pound together in a pestle and mortar. Alternatively, mash everything together with a dinner fork. Once you have a smooth paste, spread thinly on triangles or wide soldiers of hot buttered toast.
Squeeze of lemon juice	
Tip of a teaspoon cayenne pepper	
Freshly ground black pepper	
Hot buttered toast, to serve	

It's also good spread thinly on toast and served with scrambled egg or spread sparingly onto hot buttered crumpets.

It will store, covered, in the fridge for a few days. A small amount is a flavoursome addition to a shepherd's pie, particularly if it's made with lamb: about ¼–½ teaspoon is plenty, and don't add any salt!

TUNA MELT

Drain the tuna and use some of the oil to fry the potatoes. Put the tuna on top, season with the black pepper and heat through, stirring slightly. Make your toast, butter it lightly and arrange the potato and tuna on top, sprinkle with grated cheese and grill until golden and bubbling.

Serve with tomato ketchup.

Quantities to suit of:

Tinned tuna, preferably in oil
Leftover mashed potatoes
Freshly ground black pepper
Slices of decent bread
Butter for spreading
Grated cheese

EXTRA ENERGY-GIVING PEANUT BUTTER ON TOAST

This is just right if you are flagging a bit by lunchtime. Lightly toast the bread. Meanwhile, mix the seeds and peanut butter together and, once the toast is ready, spread it over. This is particularly good with a glass of orange juice.

✓ **Useful Note** The same seeds are really good mixed in with your morning muesli to give you extra energy to face the day ahead. A few dried cranberries and some sliced apple or banana as well will really set you up.

1–2 slices wholemeal bread, preferably wholegrain
Peanut butter, crunchy or smooth
Selection of seeds such as pumpkin, sunflower, linseed, hemp

CINNAMON TOAST

This is a lovely old-fashioned teatime treat. Best eaten tucked up in front of the fire or huddled over a pot of tea in the kitchen.

Quantities to suit of:

Slices from a decent loaf, cut fairly thinly, brown or white
Butter for spreading
Equal quantities of ground cinnamon and unrefined sugar mixed together (caster or granulated sugar are both suitable)

Toast the bread lightly, cool slightly and butter (it should be actual butter as this is key to the flavour). Sprinkle the sugar and cinnamon mixture over the top and put under a hot grill until bubbling. Cut into triangles and *cool slightly before eating*, otherwise you will have the roof of your mouth off!

GARLIC MUSHROOMS ON TOAST

Quantity of button, closed cap or chestnut mushrooms, or a mixture
Butter or oil for frying, or a mixture
Finely sliced garlic clove

Slice the mushrooms and fry gently in the butter or oil. Don't let them overcook or shrink. Add the garlic towards the end of the cooking time.

Serve with triangles of hot buttered toast or quick garlic bread (see page 127) and a little greenery. A little chopped parsley or snipped chives scattered over the top looks appetising.

CREAMED MUSHROOMS ON TOAST

Wholegrain bread makes the best toast for this. A little green salad on the side makes more of a meal and a few snipped chives fancy it up a bit.

Heat some oil in a pan and cook the mushrooms over a moderate heat: put a lid on the pan so that the mushrooms half fry, half steam until they are soft and succulent. Add the garlic towards the end of the cooking time. Once the mushrooms and garlic are cooked through, stir in the cream and turn up the heat so that the cream bubbles and reduces and darkens in colour slightly, stirring throughout. Season with black pepper and salt.

Serve with triangles of toast.

Oil, for frying
250g (9oz) mushrooms, closed cap, button, chestnut or a mixture, sliced
I finely chopped garlic clove, or a little minced garlic from a jar
6 tablespoons or so of double cream
Freshly ground black pepper and a touch of sea salt

CHICKEN LIVERS ON TOAST

It is possible to get free range chicken livers: ask your local butcher.

Chicken livers Butter or oil for frying Finely sliced garlic, if liked A little salt and freshly ground black pepper to serve	Separate the livers: remove any bits you don't like the look of, and put the livers into a hot pan with the butter and/or oil. Fry gently, turning and moving them round the pan very carefully. If using garlic, add it to the pan halfway through. Don't overcook the livers. They should be light brown in colour with just a slightly pink colour inside. Season lightly to taste and serve on hot buttered toast. You may like to add a few gentle shakes of Worcestershire sauce, and a little greenery on the side would be nice.

QUICK BOSTON STYLE BEANS

SERVES 2 but it's easy to increase the quantities 1 small onion Oil for frying Small amount of fresh chilli or pinch of chilli powder 1 clove of garlic or a little minced garlic from a jar (optional) 415g tin of baked beans 1 rounded teaspoon black treacle 1 teaspoon of fairly mild mustard: either wholegrain or French	Fry the onion in a little oil with the chilli, if using, and the garlic. Add the beans and stir in the black treacle and the mustard. Simmer gently until cooked through and all the flavours have amalgamated. Eat with plenty of fairly thickly cut buttered toast. For a more substantial dish you can add some bacon or sausages (or both) and serve with baked potatoes. You could snip the bacon into pieces and fry and scatter over the beans at the last moment or you could stir it in. Cook the sausages separately and serve them on the side or slice them and stir them into the beans. Alternatively, this is very good with some leftover slices of cold pork.

Quick Curried Beans

Stir a little **curry paste**, such as Madras, into **a tin of beans** and add **a handful of sultanas**. Heat through and serve with **buttered toast**. You could also add a dollop of thick plain yoghurt and a little lime pickle on the side.

Eggs and Toast

No section on toast would be complete without at least a mention of eggs. Here are more detailed instructions for scrambled eggs and just a few hints for poached and boiled. For Fried Eggs, see the Breakfasts section.

Scrambled Eggs

These two versions of scrambled eggs make great light lunch or supper dishes. The smoked salmon one also makes a lovely special breakfast. If you would prefer plain scrambled eggs just follow either of the recipes below, without adding the leeks or the smoked salmon.

SCRAMBLED EGGS WITH LEEKS

Leeks

Knob or two of butter

New-laid eggs, lightly
   beaten (not whisked to
   a froth)

Small splash of milk

Salt and pepper to taste

It's difficult to give precise quantities here: 2–3 eggs per person and one medium leek, or equivalent, would be about right. Peel and clean the leeks, slice, and either steam or soften in butter. Drain on kitchen paper. Melt a little butter in a pan and pour in the eggs and milk. Season lightly.

Try not to stir too briskly but rather shuffle the eggs gently round the pan: a flat-ended wooden spatula works better than a spoon. Once the eggs are starting to scramble, add the leeks and continue cooking until the eggs are scrambled to your liking.

Serve with triangles of hot buttered toast, possibly a little bacon, and a spot of brown sauce, if liked.

SCRAMBLED EGGS WITH SMOKED SALMON

Knob of butter

New-laid eggs, lightly
   beaten

Small splash of milk

Smoked salmon

Freshly ground black
   pepper (you won't need
   salt)

Again, use quantities to suit. Melt the butter in the pan and add the beaten eggs and milk. Stir gently, as above. Once the eggs are almost ready, snip in some strips of salmon, cutting it straight into the pan with kitchen scissors. Season with a couple of grinds of black pepper. Don't add the salmon too soon or it will overcook, becoming a dull pale pink rather than translucent, and the flavour will be ruined.

Serve with triangles of hot buttered toast or lightly toasted bagels.

EXTRA LIGHT AND LUSCIOUS VERSION

Instead of a splash of milk, add a generous teaspoon of half fat crème fraiche to the eggs. This is especially good with the smoked salmon. When you first add it, it will look a bit blobby, but don't worry, it will soon disappear once the mixture warms up.

POACHED EGGS ON TOAST

Poached eggs on toast are such a comforting and nourishing light lunch or supper: the white should be firm but the yolk runny so that it can run all over the toast when you put your knife in. It's easier to poach eggs in an actual egg poacher. You can tell when they are done much more easily. You can see them clearly when you take the lid off and give them a gentle nudge with the tip of a dinner knife.

If you can get hold of one, a stainless steel egg poacher with stainless steel cups works brilliantly: non-stick cups are inclined to scratch easily and plastic cups are forever melting when you get them too near the hob by mistake.

Fill your egg poacher halfway up with boiling water from the kettle. Put a little dot of butter into each cup and put the lid back on. Once the water has come back to the boil and the butter has melted crack the eggs in. Put the lid on and cook for roughly the time it takes to make your toast: about three minutes.

Once the egg is cooked the white will be opaque and will come away from the side of the cup easily when nudged with a knife; it will still be quite 'quivery' though. Slip a dinner knife round the edges of the cups (unless they are non-stick) and turn the eggs out onto slices of buttered toast. Eat immediately.

BOILED EGGS

Whilst soft-boiled eggs should be as fresh as possible, hard-boiled eggs are better when they are a few days old. The white sets better and they are much easier to peel.

It's amazing that something as simple as a boiled egg should attract so much argument as to which is the best way to do it. This is one method but it's certainly not the only way. Ideally, the eggs should be at room temperature.

Realistically, four eggs are the most you can boil at a time, if they are to be eaten with a soft and runny yolk and firm whites. Bring the water to a boil in a small to medium sized deep saucepan. Put in your eggs: a spaghetti server is a handy tool for the job. Start timing from the moment they go into the boiling water. An average size egg should take 4 minutes and it's best if you don't actually cut the top off the eggs until you have buttered the toast, which just gives the whites a fraction longer to set. Bantam eggs may only need 3½ minutes. Eat immediately with toast soldiers for dipping.

Soft-Boiled Eggs

Soft-boiled eggs are also lovely with steamed florets of purple sprouting broccoli or asparagus spears dipped into them.

Boiled eggs make a gorgeous light lunch or tea with new brown bread and butter and some really fresh watercress on the side, with just a tiny bit of Maldon Salt for dipping. Make a pot of tea and have some home-made strawberry jam on the table to have with the rest of your bread and butter.

Eggs Mollet or 'Oeufs Mollets'

This is a soft-boiled egg, but peeled and eaten warm, rather than eaten from an egg cup with a spoon. You can serve it as you might a poached egg. One of these is great on a freshly baked bap with some ham: see **Ham Knuckle** in the Light Lunches and Midweek Suppers section.

Hard-Boiled Eggs

Hard-boiled eggs can be a nasty, rubbery, sulphurous, dark-ringed nightmare! Alternatively, they can be a lovely delicate treat. To avoid the first scenario, boil for 7–8 minutes, *no longer*, and then plunge into cold water *immediately*. Crack them, then roll them briskly over a work surface a couple of times and try to peel the shell off in one go.

Cakes

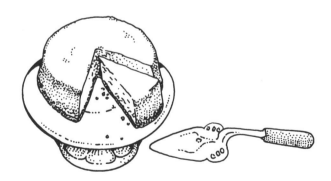

Cake Surgery

Here are a few helpful suggestions for when things seem to be going wrong. It is very easy to blame yourself when a cake doesn't work. The most common failure seems to be **the sponge that doesn't rise**. Quite often someone has an experience with a flat sponge and assumes they are totally responsible, completely lacking in some kind of instinctive gift for cake making. They lose all heart and never try again. This is a shame as more than likely one or more of the following is the cause.

Flour

Tired self-raising flour is a common reason for a failed sponge. If you are using self-raising flour for a recipe it needs to be *completely fresh*. It should be well within its sell by date and it also helps if the bag has not been opened for very long. It must also be stored properly in a cool dry place; not by the cooker, for example, or by the window. Most people seem to be aware that dried herbs and spices deteriorate quickly: this is also the case with self-raising flour. The raising agents in the flour lose their effectiveness after a while. Don't stockpile great big 1.5kg bags of self-raising flour: buy just one 500g bag at a time. A 500g bag is, on average, sufficient for two and a half cakes If you bake regularly you will probably only make one cake a week that needs self-raising flour, so buy little and often as you need it.

Correct oven temperature and times

This is another common cause of failure and an area where you will almost certainly have to resort to trial and error. Keep a note of the times and temperatures you have used for particular recipes, then you will know when you come to make those recipes again.

Generally speaking, if you follow a recipe to the letter and your ingredients are fresh you will have good results. The majority of recipes will work even if the cooking temperature is a few degrees adrift. However, there are some recipes, and sponge cake is one of them, where exact temperature and consistency of temperature is absolutely crucial.

Ovens can, and do, vary in temperature: 200°C on the dial does not necessarily mean a temperature of 200°C inside the oven. If you are having difficulty with your baking, it is worth getting an oven thermometer and checking. You might find your oven is set hotter than it indicates: in other words, the dial says 200°C but the temperature is actually 220°C. In which case, if a recipe says cook something at 220°C you would set *your* oven to 200°C. Most likely you would set the oven to 180°C if the recipe stated 200°C and so on.

You might also find you have to vary your cooking times from those stated in recipes. If your oven runs on the hot side, for example, and has a powerful fan, you may need a shorter cooking time. It is worth noting here that fan ovens generally do seem hotter as the hot air circulates round the food: the difference is usually about 20 degrees centigrade.

Eggs must be very fresh

Fresh eggs really do make a better cake. As an egg gets older its composition changes and the components that help the cake to rise deteriorate and eventually stop working.

Use warmed, softened butter

Butter gives a lovely flavour and texture. It must be soft and slightly warm to mix properly. If you try to mix it in when it is cold and too hard the cake will be heavy. An easy way to soften butter quickly is to put it in the microwave on High for 20–30 seconds. Some people swear by block margarine but soft spreadable margarine isn't suitable.

Use the right type of sugar

Unless the recipe specifically gives a choice, use the type of sugar stipulated. Caster sugar is best for light sponge cakes as it is much finer.

Correct mixing

Generally, with some notable exceptions such as muffins, cakes need to be thoroughly mixed. However, this doesn't mean you should over-mix: be thorough but don't overdo it. Mix sponge cakes until the mixture looks smooth and glossy, then ease it gently into the baking tin(s). Even if you are using a food processor, try to add the ingredients in the same stages you would if you were mixing by hand, rather than the all-in-one method some people prefer. This means whizz the butter and sugar together first until they are combined and fluffy, then sieve a layer of flour over them, next add the eggs (already beaten lightly with a fork), finally add the rest of the flour and after a quick whizz, extra liquid, such as milk, if you are using any.

Sieve your flour

Modern flour is beautifully fine but it does settle in the bag and you need to aerate it again. This is why you need to sieve it: to let lots of air in so you end up with a light, well-risen cake. Hold your sieve quite a way above the bowl if you can. (Icing sugar, on the other hand, needs sieving to remove any lumps, so it is perfectly fine to push icing sugar through the sieve with a spoon.)

Correct size tins

You must use the same size tin as stipulated in the recipe. The cooking times have been worked out around a particular tin size so if you use something different it won't cook at the same rate.

Don't open the oven door while baking is in progress!

Every time you open your oven door, you lose heat. It is particularly crucial that you don't lose heat when you are baking something that needs to rise, such as a sponge cake, Yorkshire pudding or soufflé. If you have a window in your oven door, make use of it to check on progress. If you do have to return a cake to the oven because it's not quite done, be aware that it won't be quite as good as if it had been undisturbed for the whole baking time, and make a note for next time.

Finally, here is a *completely fictional* account of how one woman just couldn't seem to get the hang of it!

Mrs S	So, how did you get on with the chocolate cake recipe?
Friend	It was a complete disaster. I told you I wouldn't be able to do it.
Mrs S	Oh dear! Did you follow the recipe exactly?
Friend	Of course I did! Well, more or less.
Mrs S	The flour was fresh?
Friend	Well, it was the same flour my sister used for Gran's 80th birthday cake, and that turned out all right.
Mrs S	You don't mean the same *actual bag*, do you? Your Gran's 80th was last year!
Friend	Yes, I thought it would be all right.
Mrs S	Well, no, not really; it would be *a little bit* out of date by now! Did you soften the butter?
Friend	No need! I used that soft olive oil spready thing instead from that special diet I was on.
Mrs S	Ah, I see. And the eggs? They were fresh?
Friend	Oh, yes! They were the organic ones from the Farmers' Market! Only the best!
Mrs S	Um, the Farmers' Market was two weeks ago! What about the cocoa, did you use that good-quality one I mentioned, with the lovely flavour?
Friend	Oh, yes! Well, actually, it was their drinking chocolate, but it wouldn't matter, would it?
Mrs S	Oh dear. Well, yes, I'm afraid it would. Did you mix it all until it was smooth and glossy?
Friend	Smooth and glossy? Oh, I don't know about that, I didn't have my lenses in.
Mrs S	The tins? Did you use two tins, the size I recommended?

Friend	Well, no, I may have slipped up there. I only had one tin but it was quite big so I just shoved it all in together.
Mrs S	Right. I see. So the cooking times would be completely out then.
Friend	Someone came to the door as a matter of fact, and I forgot to set the timer anyway. I just kept opening the oven door and testing it with a cocktail stick, like you said. Are you all right? For a minute there I thought you were crying!

Oven temperatures

Please be aware that individual oven performance can vary tremendously. An average temperature of 160–180ºC or equivalent has been suggested for most recipes in this section. Some ovens may need to be set higher or lower.

SPONGE CAKES

This is a classic Victoria type sponge cake recipe. All sponge cakes of this type contain equal amounts of self-raising flour, butter and caster sugar. The eggs, still in their shells, should weigh close to that amount as well. This used to be known, in the days before metrication, as a 'six-ounce mix'. An 'eight-ounce mix' is also often used. Theoretically, you can make the mix any weight you like as long as the ingredients all weigh the same. You would have to work out the corresponding tin sizes and cooking times as well, though.

Unlike pastry, where everything needs to be cold, when making sponge cakes everything needs to be slightly warm. Take the eggs out of the fridge beforehand and warm the butter slightly in the microwave if necessary.

Oven temperatures for sponge cakes

Suggested temperatures for baking sponge cakes of this type can vary from160ºC to 190ºC.

If your oven is a fairly steady average performer, set it to 170–180ºC. If you have a very fierce oven, 160ºC may be preferable.

If the finished sponge comes out of the oven flat and hard, it is likely the temperature was too high and the top cooked before the centre could rise.

If the sponge comes out of the oven heavy and not completely cooked, it is likely that the temperature was too low or it wasn't cooked for long enough.

It may be you will have to have a couple of attempts before you get it right, but don't give up: keep notes and persevere; you will get there in the end!

PLAIN AND SIMPLE SPONGE CAKE

175g (6oz) self raising
  flour
175g (6oz) butter
175g (6oz) unrefined
  caster sugar
2–3 eggs, as fresh as
  possible, combined
  weight 175g (6oz) or a
  little over
2 tablespoons of milk

Good quality jam such as
  seedless raspberry or
  bramble jelly
  (strawberry can be a bit
  sweet to fill a sweet
  sponge cake)

Icing sugar to finish

Preheat oven to 180ºC (fan oven) or equivalent, see below.

Grease two 18cm (7in) loose-bottomed sandwich tins.

Whizz the butter and sugar together in a food processor until light and fluffy. Sieve the flour in carefully and add the eggs. Whizz again. Add the milk and whizz until very smooth and glossy and everything is well mixed.

You may need to scrape the mixture down from the sides a couple of times with a flexible spatula. You should now have a dropping consistency. That is to say, the mixture isn't so thick that it won't drop easily off a spoon, but it isn't runny either.

Pour into the prepared cake tins using a flexible spatula to help all the mixture out.

Bake in the middle of the oven for 18–20 minutes until the cakes are risen and golden and a skewer inserted comes out clean.

Allow the cakes to rest for a few moments and then carefully loosen the edges with a small palette knife.

If the tins are too hot to handle, stand the cakes, one at a time, on a jar or something similar. Using both hands, protected with an oven glove or tea towel, pull the side of the tin down so the cake is left, still on its base, on top of the jar. Move it closer to your cooling rack and losen from the base using a large palette knife. Transfer gently (you may need a fish slice as well as the palette knife at this stage) onto the cooling rack. Repeat with the other cake.

Try not to flip the cake over straight out of the tin onto the cooling rack. This manoeuvre will leave you with deep lines or squares indented across the top of your cake which doesn't look very professional.

Once the cakes are cool, spread with jam, position the other on top, and sieve icing sugar over it. (White castor sugar is more traditional but it can feel a bit too gritty in contrast with the light texture of the sponge.)

Light Lemon Sponge

Add the very finely grated zest of half a lemon to the plain sponge cake recipe above.

Once the cake has cooled, fill with **Lemon Buttercream** (see below) and sieve some icing sugar over the top.

Lemon Buttercream

Beat the butter until creamy in a roomy bowl. Sieve in the icing sugar, a little at a time. Finally, stir in the lemon juice just to loosen it slightly.	50g (2oz) softened butter 110g (4oz) icing sugar 1–2 tablespoons lemon juice

Old-Fashioned Birthday Cake

This is a really simple, old-fashioned, cake-shaped birthday cake.
Make the plain sponge cake as above. Sandwich with jam and ice the top with the glacé icing below.

Sieve the icing sugar into a large bowl and stir in the lemon juice. Beat with a wooden spoon until smooth and glossy.	**For the glacé icing**
	175g (6oz) icing sugar
Spoon the icing carefully over the cake: aim to keep it all on top of the cake but if a little drizzles down the sides, don't worry; it will just look more traditional, like a cake in a child's picture book.	3 tablespoons lemon juice
For **Pink Icing**, see page 147.	

Sponge Cake with Jam and Buttercream

Again, make a perfectly simple sponge cake, as above, spread the lower half with jam and then carefully spread lemon buttercream, as above, over the top of the jam, using a small palette knife. Put the top cake on and sieve icing sugar over it.

CHOCOLATE CAKE

This makes a lovely birthday cake for older children and grown-ups too.

175g (6oz) softened butter
175g (6oz) unrefined
   caster sugar
150g (5oz) self-raising
   flour
3 eggs
25g (1oz) good-quality
   cocoa powder (not
   drinking chocolate)
2 tablespoons milk

Preheat oven to 180°C (fan oven) or equivalent.

Grease two 18cm (7in) loose-bottomed sandwich tins.

Whizz the butter and sugar together in a food processor until combined and fluffy. Sieve some of the flour in a layer over the mixture and then add the eggs. Sieve in the rest of the flour and the cocoa. Whizz again. Add the milk and whizz until smooth and glossy.

You may need to remove the lid a couple of times and scrape the mixture down from the sides with a flexible spatula.

Turn into the greased sandwich tins and bake for 18–20 minutes or until nicely risen and firm but springy to the touch. A wooden cocktail stick inserted into the cakes should come out clean.

Allow the cakes to rest for a few moments and then carefully loosen the edges with a small palette knife. If the tins are too hot to handle, stand the cakes, one at a time, on a jar or something similar. Using both hands, pull the side of the tin down so the cake is left, still on its base, on top of the jar. Move it closer to your cooling rack and loosen from the base using a large palette knife. Transfer gently (you may need a fish slice as well as the palette knife at this stage) onto the cooling rack. Repeat with the other cake.

CHOCOLATE BUTTERCREAM

Sieve the combined cocoa and icing sugar into the softened butter, a little at a time, mixing it all together with a wooden spoon. Finally, loosen the mixture slightly with the milk and beat until smooth and glossy.

Spread some of the buttercream carefully onto one of the sponges with a small palette knife, put the second sponge on top and spread the rest of the buttercream over it.

You might like to grate some chocolate over the top to decorate. If you would like to ice the top with chocolate glacé icing instead, see **Little Chocolate Cakes**, on page 148.

25g (1oz) good-quality cocoa powder
150g (5oz) icing sugar
75g (3oz) butter, softened
A little milk to mix

ALL SORTS OF FAIRY CAKES AND BUTTERFLY CAKES

Children love these, but then again, so do adults. They are the perfect cake for children to practise baking on and great for children's parties, picnics and afternoon tea.

The mixture is exactly the same as the sponge cake mixture and the same rules apply: it is best to have everything slightly warm, so leave the eggs out of the fridge and warm the butter slightly in the microwave if necessary; 10–20 seconds or so on High is usually just about right.

ICED FAIRY CAKES

You can have fun decorating these with various bits and pieces: coloured chocolate bean sweets, hundreds and thousands, crystallised rose petals and violets, and so on.

Another lovely thing you can do is to decorate them with real flowers from the garden, when available, but arrange them on the cakes just before serving. Stick with something you know is harmless such as primroses, pansies or violas, calendula (pot marigold) petals, borage flowers and rose petals. Sit them on kitchen paper first for a while if they are a bit damp. Be sure not to use anything that has been sprayed or is close to an exhaust-fume-laden road.

MAKES about 18 cakes	Preheat oven to 180°C (fan ovens) or equivalent.

175g (6oz) softened butter
175g (6oz) unrefined caster sugar
175g (6oz) self-raising flour
3 eggs
2 tablespoons milk

You will need a 12-cup muffin tin plus paper cases

Whizz the butter and sugar together in a food processor until combined and fluffy. Sieve in some of the flour and add the eggs, sieve in the rest of the flour. Whizz again. Add the milk and whizz until smooth and glossy. You may need to scrape the mixture down from the sides a couple of times with a flexible spatula.

Arrange the paper cases in the muffin tin and spoon two generous teaspoons of mixture into each case. Bake for around 15 minutes or until risen and pale golden and springy to the touch. A skewer or wooden cocktail stick should come out clean when inserted. Remove from the tin with a small palette knife and cool on a wire rack. Bake the remaining part batch.

✔ **Note** This will give you muffin-shaped fairy cakes with rounded tops. If you want a flatter, more cup cake size, fill each case barely halfway and once in the oven check after 12 minutes or so. You should have enough mixture left over for about another half dozen cakes.

GLACÉ ICING

The lemon juice takes the edge off the sweetness.

Sieve the icing sugar into a large bowl and stir in the lemon juice. Beat with a wooden spoon until glossy.

Spoon the icing over the cooled cakes. You can either spread the icing over the whole top of the cake, cup cake style, or spoon on a little circle of icing in the middle of each cake.

225g (8oz) icing sugar
2 tablespoons lemon juice
(sieve through a tea
strainer)

PINK ICING

For pink-tinted icing without using food colouring, add a little sieved raspberry jam. For a more lilac-toned pink use a little touch of blackberry jelly or sieved blackcurrant jam.

TEENY TINY FAIRY CAKES

These are exactly the same as the Fairy Cakes above but half the size. Make up the mixture and icing in exactly the same way but bake in two 12-cup mini muffin tins instead, and then a second batch, using petits fours cases. They will take less time to bake, usually about 8–10 minutes.

CURRANT FAIRY CAKES

Make up the fairy cake mixture as above and once it is all mixed together remove the processor blade and *stir* in 75–110g (3–4oz) of currants (depending on how curranty you want the cakes). Stir them into the mixture because if you whizz them in the processor you will get a horrible grey sludge as all the currants are whizzed to a pulp. (Obviously, I have never done this myself!)

These are lovely plain but possibly even better iced with glacé icing.

BUTTERFLY CAKES

These little cakes look so pretty and delicate. Make up the fairy cake mixture, as above, filling the cases ¾ full. Make up some **Lemon Buttercream**.

Once the cakes are cool slice the tops off and put to one side. Spoon a little dollop of buttercream onto each cake. Cut each top in half so you have two 'wings' and arrange on top of each cake. Just before you want to eat them, sieve some icing sugar over the top: if you do it too soon the icing sugar will eventually sink into the cake.

LEMON BUTTERCREAM

50g (2oz) softened butter 110g (4oz) icing sugar 1–2 tablespoons lemon juice	Beat the butter until creamy in a largish bowl. Sieve in the icing sugar, a little at a time. Finally, stir in the lemon juice to loosen the mixture slightly.

LITTLE CHOCOLATE CAKES

MAKES about 18 cakes	Preheat oven to 180ºC (fan oven) or equivalent.

175g (6oz) softened butter
175g (6oz) unrefined
  caster sugar
150g (5oz) self-raising
  flour
3 eggs
25g (1oz) good-quality
  cocoa powder (not
  drinking chocolate)
2 tablespoons milk
	Whizz the butter and sugar together in a food processor until combined and fluffy. Sieve some of the flour in a layer over the mixture and then add the eggs. Sieve in the rest of the flour and the cocoa. Whizz again. Add the milk and whizz until smooth and glossy. You may need to remove the lid a couple of times and scrape the mixture down from the sides with a flexible spatula.

You will need a 12-cup
  muffin tin plus paper
  cases
	Arrange the paper cases in the muffin tin and spoon two fairly generous teaspoons of mixture into each case. Bake for around 15 minutes or until domed and risen and springy to the touch. A skewer or wooden cocktail stick should come out clean when inserted. Remove from the tin with a small palette knife and leave to cool on a wire rack. Bake the remaining part batch.

CHOCOLATE GLACÉ ICING

Sieve about a quarter of the icing sugar and cocoa powder into a large bowl and stir in the milk. Sieve the rest of the icing sugar and cocoa in, a little at a time, until it is all incorporated. Beat with a wooden spoon until glossy. Spoon over the cooled cakes. You can either spread the icing over the whole top of the cake, cup cake style, or spoon a little circle of icing into the middle of each cake.

You might like to decorate the top of the Little Chocolate Cakes with a single Maltesers® chocolate ball. These are just a fraction too big and look nice and comical, like a picture book cake with a cherry on top!

Maltesers is a registered trademark of Mars

200g (7oz) icing sugar
25g (1oz) cocoa powder
3–4 tablespoons milk

CHOCOLATE BUTTERFLY CAKES

*The above mixture also makes great butterfly cakes. You can make them with either **Chocolate Buttercream** (below) or **Lemon and Vanilla Buttercream Icing** (see **Banana Buns** on page 151). It's quite nice if you are having a bit of a party to make half with chocolate and half with vanilla and arrange them on the same plate. If you need to soften the butter quickly, try putting it in the microwave on High for 10–20 seconds.*

Sieve the combined cocoa and icing sugar into the softened butter, a little at a time, mixing it all together with a wooden spoon. Finally, loosen the mixture slightly with the milk and beat until smooth and glossy.

Once the cakes are cool slice the tops off and put to one side. Spoon a little dollop of buttercream onto each cake. Cut each top in half so you have two 'wings' and arrange on top of each cake. Just before you want to eat them, sieve some icing sugar over the top: if you do it too soon the icing sugar will eventually sink into the cake.

For the chocolate buttercream

25g (1oz) good-quality cocoa powder
150g (5oz) icing sugar
75g (3oz) butter, softened
A little milk to mix

EASY, ADAPTABLE AND DELICIOUS CAKES AND BUNS

The following recipes are all very similar in approach. You can make one large cake to cut at or a dozen little buns instead: sometimes individual buns seem more popular than a single cake. The other advantage of buns is they are much quicker to bake.

Note 'Cover loosely with greaseproof paper' means just tear off a piece long enough to wrap loosely round the tin and tuck underneath it to secure, just enough to protect the top from burning but not so tightly that the cake sticks to the paper as it rises.

BANANA CAKE

The bananas for this recipe need to be just overripe: the skins should be a bit speckled and the banana should look slightly mealy but still be white. Don't be tempted to add any more banana 'just to use it up' as too much banana will make the cake solid and heavy.

110g (4oz) softened butter
110g (4oz) soft light
  brown sugar
110g (4oz) wholemeal
  flour
50g (2oz) plain flour
50g (2oz) ground almonds
2 teaspoons baking
  powder
2 fresh eggs
150–175g (5–6oz) ripe
  bananas, peeled weight,
  mashed to a purée but
  not liquidy
	Preheat oven to 160ºC (fan oven) or equivalent.
	
	Grease an 18cm (7in) loose-bottomed cake tin.
	
	Whizz the butter and sugar together in a food processor. Add the flours, ground almonds, baking powder and eggs and whizz until combined. Finally, add the banana and whizz that in too. Spoon into the prepared tin, cover loosely with greaseproof paper and bake for about 1¼ hours, or until a skewer inserted into the cake comes out clean. If you have a fierce oven, test after an hour. Loosen the sides and bottom with a palette knife, remove from the tin and cool on a wire rack.

Banana Buns

You might prefer to make banana buns instead: for some strange reason these are guaranteed to disappear twice as fast! All you do is make the mixture as above but spoon it into a greased 12-cup muffin tin instead. (There is no need to cover with greaseproof paper.) Bake at the same temperature as above for 20 minutes, or until the buns are springy to the touch and a skewer comes out clean.

Optional icing
Both the cake and buns are lovely as they are but sometimes you might like to top them off with a buttercream icing. The vanilla in the following recipe goes beautifully with the banana and the lemon juice just takes the edge off the sweetness.

Lemon and Vanilla Buttercream Icing

Cream the butter in a bowl large enough to give you room to manoeuvre. Use a wooden spoon. Gradually add the icing sugar, passing it through a sieve. When the icing sugar is all combined, add the vanilla and stir in a squeeze of lemon juice, just enough to loosen the mixture slightly.

Spread over the top of the cake or buns. A few dried banana chips make a good decoration.

50g (2oz) softened butter
110g (4oz) icing sugar
Few drops of vanilla extract or ¼ teaspoon of vanilla bean paste
Squeeze of lemon juice

CARROT CAKE

*As you will see this is very similar to the **Banana Cake**. Unsurprisingly, the quality of the carrots is crucial to the flavour: you want fresh, young, fairly small carrots, nothing tired, old or overlarge. The cinnamon gives a hint of warmth and depth and the orange zest a lovely freshness.*

110g (4oz) softened butter
110g (4oz) soft brown
    sugar
50g (2oz) plain flour
110g (4oz) wholemeal
    flour
50g (2oz) ground almonds
2 teaspoons baking
    powder
1 teaspoon ground
    cinnamon
2 eggs
150g (5oz) grated carrot
    (grated weight)
Finely grated zest of 1
    orange

Preheat oven to 160ºC (fan oven) or equivalent.

Grease an 18cm (7in) loose-bottomed cake tin.

Whizz the butter and sugar together in a food processor. Add flours, ground almonds, baking powder, cinnamon and eggs and whizz until combined. Finally, add the grated carrot and orange zest and whizz again. Spoon into the prepared tin, cover loosely with greaseproof paper and bake for about 1¼ hours, or until a skewer inserted into the cake comes out clean. If you have a fierce oven, test after an hour. Loosen the sides and bottom with a palette knife, remove from tin and cool on a wire rack.

CARROT BUNS

This recipe also makes brilliant buns. Make the recipe as above but spoon into a greased 12-cup muffin tin instead. There is no need to cover. Bake at the above temperature for 20 minutes or until a skewer comes out clean.

Optional icing
Again, both the cake and buns are lovely on their own, but icing *is* usually required for carrot cake. Instead of the traditional cream cheese frosting try this light buttercream version instead.

ORANGE BUTTERCREAM ICING

Cream the butter in a bowl large enough to give you room to manoeuvre. Use a wooden spoon. Gradually add the icing sugar, passing it through a sieve. When the icing sugar is all combined, stir in the orange juice, just enough to loosen the mixture slightly.

Spread onto the top of the cake or buns.

50g (2oz) softened butter
110g (4oz) icing sugar
Squeeze of orange juice

LIGHT APPLE CAKE

This apple version of the above cakes is lovely and light. It's perfect as it is or with a little glacé icing drizzled in zigzag lines across the top.

Preheat oven to 160°C (fan oven) or equivalent.

Grease an 18cm (7in) loose-bottomed cake tin.

Whizz the butter and sugar together in a food processor. Add flour, ground almonds, baking powder and eggs and whizz until combined. Finally, add the apple and whizz. Spoon into the prepared tin, cover loosely with greaseproof paper and bake for about 1¼ hours, or until a skewer inserted into the cake comes out clean. If you have a fierce oven, test after an hour. Loosen the sides and bottom with a palette knife, remove from the tin and cool on a wire rack.

110g (4oz) softened butter
110g (4oz) soft brown sugar
175g (6oz) plain flour
50g (2oz) ground almonds
2 teaspoons baking powder
2 eggs
175g (6oz) finely chopped and peeled apple

APPLE BUNS

This recipe also makes nice little buns. Make the mixture as above but spoon into a greased 12-cup muffin tin instead. There is no need to cover. Bake at the above temperature for 20 minutes or until a skewer comes out clean.

As before, both the cake and buns are just fine as they are but occasionally an iced version is welcome. This time, a glacé icing seems called for rather than buttercream.

Optional lemon glacé icing

110g (4oz) icing sugar
1–2 tablespoons lemon juice

Sieve the icing sugar into a bowl and stir in a tablespoon or two of lemon juice – make a fairly stiff mixture so that when you put it on top of the cake or buns it drizzles slightly over the side but doesn't run off it completely!

APPLE AND CINNAMON BUNS

*Now for something really special! These buns are just lovely as they are but they are **fabulous** with a topping of vanilla and cinnamon buttercream! You can use 2 teaspoons of baking powder instead of the bicarbonate of soda and cream of tartar if you prefer, but the end result is not as airy and fluffy.*

Preheat oven to 160ºC (fan oven) or equivalent.

Grease a 12-cup muffin tin.

Whizz the butter and sugar together in a food processor. Add the flour, ground almonds, bicarbonate of soda and cream of tartar, cinnamon and eggs and whizz until combined. Next, add the 175g (6 oz) of chopped apple and whizz. Finally, remove the blade from your processor, scrape any mixture back into the bowl and stir in the 50g (2 oz) of diced apple. Spoon into the prepared tin and bake for about 20 minutes, or until a skewer inserted into the buns comes out clean. Leave the buns in the tin for five minutes or so to cool slightly (they are quite fragile at this stage and break easily) before loosening with a small palette knife. Remove from the tin and finish cooling on a wire rack.

110g (4 oz) softened butter
110g (4 oz) unrefined caster sugar
175g (6 oz) plain flour
50g (2 oz) ground almonds
1 teaspoon bicarbonate of soda
2 teaspoons cream of tartar
1 teaspoon powdered cinnamon
2 eggs
175g (6 oz) finely chopped and peeled apple
Plus: an additional 50g (2 oz) diced and peeled apple

Vanilla and Cinnamon Buttercream Icing

50g (2oz) softened butter
110g (4oz) icing sugar
1 teaspoon powdered cinnamon
Few drops of vanilla extract or ¼ teaspoon of vanilla bean paste
Squeeze of lemon juice

Cream the butter in a bowl large enough to give you room to manoeuvre using a wooden spoon. Sieve the icing sugar and cinnamon together and add to the butter in batches, stirring each batch in thoroughly before you add the next. When the icing sugar and cinnamon is all combined, add the vanilla and stir in a squeeze of lemon juice, just enough to loosen the mixture slightly. Spoon a little onto the top of each bun and finish off with a little sprinkle of cinnamon.

Strawberry Cake

*This is a beautiful summery recipe. It is very handy if you are lucky enough to have a glut of strawberries in the garden but if you haven't, it's worth buying some especially for it as it is so delicious! The cake and buns (see below) are both lovely topped off with the **Lemon and Vanilla Buttercream** (see page 151) or leave them plain. If you are making buns you can always ice half of them so everyone has a choice.*

110g (4oz) softened butter
75g (3oz) unrefined caster sugar
175g (6oz) plain flour
2 teaspoons baking powder
2 eggs, beaten
A few drops of good-quality vanilla extract or a dab of vanilla bean paste
50g (2oz) ground almonds
175g (6oz) strawberries, sliced

Preheat oven to 160ºC (fan oven) or equivalent.

Grease an 18cm (7in) loose-bottomed cake tin.

Whiz the butter and sugar together in a food processor. Sieve half the flour and baking powder over the mixture and add the eggs and vanilla. Add the rest of the flour and the ground almonds. Whiz again. Add the strawberries and whiz until they are all pulped and incorporated into the mixture. The mixture should now be dusky pink with the odd speck of strawberry. The gorgeous pink colour disappears after baking, which is a bit of a shame. Pour into the prepared cake tin, cover loosely with greaseproof paper and bake for 1¼ hours or until the cake is risen and golden and a skewer inserted comes out clean. Cool on a wire rack.

Strawberry Buns

If you are making buns instead of a cake, spoon the mixture into a greased 12-cup muffin tin (no need to cover) and bake for 20 minutes or until risen and golden and a skewer inserted comes out clean. Lift out with a small palette knife and cool on a wire rack.

See page 151 for *Lemon and Vanilla Buttercream*. Serve with more strawberries on the side.

Note on icings If you feel the quantity of icing suggested is a bit mean and you want to be more lavish use **75g (3oz) softened butter** to **175g (6oz) icing sugar** for the buttercream, and **175g (6oz) icing sugar** and **a spot more lemon juice** for the glacé icing.

ORANGE AND ALMOND CAKE

This cake acts as a bit of a pick-me-up: you'll feel quite perky after a slice! It is very versatile too: lovely with a cup of tea or coffee morning or afternoon, and a great breakfast with a dollop of plain yoghurt. It also makes a nice simple pudding served with Greek yoghurt or crème fraiche, and a couple of squares of dark chocolate on the side. The recipe involves boiling one of the oranges, so allow enough time.

---

2 oranges, not too large
110g (4 oz) butter softened
110g (4 oz) unrefined
   caster sugar
110g (4 oz) plain flour
110g (4 oz) ground
   almonds
2 teaspoons baking
   powder
2 eggs, beaten

You will need a greased 18cm (7in) loose-bottomed cake tin and some greaseproof paper

Preheat oven to 160ºC (fan oven) or equivalent.

Take one of the oranges, remove the little green stalk part and put it whole and unpeeled into a pan of cold water. Bring to the boil and simmer, partially covered, for about half an hour or until it is soft. Cool and cut into several pieces. Remove any pips and central pith, and any bits of membrane that will come away easily. Then put the rest into a food processor and whiz until it is an almost smooth, pale purée.

Peel or grate all the zest from the second orange (a lemon zester works best) and add to the purée. (You only need the zest of the second orange, so juice the rest immediately and drink it: cook's perk!) Add the butter and sugar and whiz until smooth. Finally, add the flour, ground almonds, baking powder and eggs and whiz until smooth and thoroughly mixed.

Pour into the prepared tin and wrap around the whole tin loosely with greaseproof paper. Bake for about 1¼ hours, or until golden on top, firm to the touch, and a skewer inserted comes out clean.

Cool on a wire rack and eat warm or cold. The cake will keep in an airtight tin for up to a week.

Extra intense and fragrant version
Seville oranges make a wonderful version of this cake. Plus, they are usually just about the right size. The season for them is quite short– from December to February – so if you can get hold of some, it's worth knowing that they freeze very well, whole, in polythene bags. You can make this cake very successfully with one frozen Seville, boiled from frozen, and the zest of a fresh orange.

Useful Note The orange used whole shouldn't be too large or the cake will be too heavy. Around about 150g (5oz) of pulped fruit is ideal. The orange for zesting can be larger, though. Also, sharper tasting oranges give a better flavour. If your oranges are very sweet, you might consider cutting the sugar down to 75g (3oz).

DORSET APPLE CAKE

This is a lovely cake for any time of year but especially in the autumn when there are so many apples around. Each cake uses 225g (half a pound) of apples, it's very easy to make and is gorgeous either warm or cold. Plenty of clotted cream is virtually obligatory.

You will need a greased loose-bottomed 20cm (8in) cake tin	225g (8oz) plain flour
	1½ teaspoons baking
Preheat oven to 160ºC (fan oven) or equivalent.	powder
	110g (4oz) butter
Sieve the flour and baking powder into a bowl and rub in the butter. Stir	110g (4oz) unrefined
in the sugar, dried fruit and apple. Mix in the eggs. Turn into the prepared	granulated sugar
tin and smooth the top with the back of a metal spoon: a wet spoon makes	75g (3oz) currants or
it easier. Sprinkle some more sugar over the top. Cover loosely with	raisins
greaseproof paper, tucking it underneath the tin to secure, and bake in a	225g (8oz) peeled, cored
preheated oven for approximately 1¼ hours, until golden on top. If you	apples, fairly finely
have a fierce oven, check after an hour.	chopped (cooking,
	eating or a mixture of
Leave in the tin for a few moments, then remove and cool on a wire rack.	both)
Store in an airtight tin.	2 eggs, lightly beaten

VIRTUOUS CAKE

This cake is sustaining but contains no fat, added sugar, or even eggs. It is very restorative with a hot cup of tea if you are feeling a bit feeble.

Note You will need to soak the dates in the tea, in a covered bowl, overnight before you start the recipe.

75g (3 oz) plain flour

3 teaspoons baking powder

2–3 teaspoons cinnamon

75g (3 oz) wholemeal flour

50g (2oz) ground almonds

175g (6oz) raisins or sultanas (or a mixture of both)

175g (6oz) dried apricot, chopped (or a mixture of dried cranberries, dried cherries, dried apricot)

225g (8oz) grated apple

225g (8 oz) dried stoned dates soaked overnight in 150ml (¼ pint) hot tea, preferably Earl Grey

Preheat oven to 160ºC (fan oven) or equivalent.

Grease a round loose-bottomed 20cm (8in) cake tin.

Sieve the plain flour with the baking powder and cinnamon into a large bowl. Stir in the wholemeal flour and ground almonds. Add the dried fruits and mix well. Add the grated apple and finally the dates and tea and stir everything together thoroughly.

Spoon the mixture (it will be very thick) into the prepared tin, smooth the top with the back of a wet metal spoon and bake in the centre of the oven for 40–45 minutes or until a skewer inserted comes out clean. Cool in the tin for a few minutes before moving to a cooling rack.

If you want to, you can also eat this fresh from the oven with custard, as a warming winter pudding.

Variation
This is a very amenable recipe: you can use desiccated coconut instead of ground almonds. Both are delicious but give a slightly different taste and texture.

COSY CAKE

This is a lovely old-fashioned cake that tastes purely of itself, nothing fancy: just fresh butter and eggs, brown sugar and fruit. It's the kind of cake your granny might bring out for Sunday tea. It is very simple to make: boiling the fruit beforehand makes it all plump and luscious and the sugar on top is the finishing touch.

You will need a greased 18cm (7in) loose-bottomed cake tin

Preheat oven to 160ºC (fan oven) or equivalent.

Cut the butter into small pieces and put into a saucepan with the water, sugar and fruit. Bring to the boil and simmer gently for 5 minutes, stirring from time to time. Leave until it is completely cold and sieve in half the flour and add the eggs; sieve the rest of the flour over the top. Mix them thoroughly together with a wooden spoon. If you use a fairly roomy saucepan you can use it to mix it all together in and save on washing up!

Pour the mixture into the prepared tin and wrap the tin loosely in greaseproof paper, tucking it underneath to secure. Bake for about 1¼ hours or until it is golden in colour and a skewer inserted comes out clean. Sprinkle with sugar while still warm.

Cool on a wire rack and store in an airtight tin.

110g (4oz) butter
200ml (scant 7fl oz) water
110g (4oz) light soft
  brown sugar
225g (8oz) dried fruit:
  currants, raisins and
  plenty of sultanas
225g (8oz) self-raising
  flour
2 eggs, lightly beaten
A teaspoonful or so of
  unrefined granulated
  sugar for sprinkling

LEMON DRIZZLE CAKE

No section on cakes is complete without a lemon drizzle cake, and this is a lovely one: not too sweet and not too sharp; moist and light. The squares work very well as part of a plate of mixed cakes with the Marmalade Squares (see below).

For the cake
110g (4oz) butter, softened
110g (4oz) unrefined
  caster sugar
175g (6oz) self-raising
  flour
2 eggs
Grated zest of 1 lemon
2 tablespoons warm water

For the drizzle
Juice of 2 lemons and 2
  level tablespoons
  unrefined caster sugar

You will need a greased 20cm (8in) square brownie tin

Preheat oven to 160ºC (fan oven) or equivalent.

Whiz the butter and sugar together until combined and fluffy. Carefully sieve in some of the flour and add the eggs, add the rest of the flour, the lemon zest and the water. Whiz until everything is mixed together but not over mixed. You may need to stop the machine a couple of times and scrape the mixture down from the sides.

Pour into the prepared tin and cover loosely with greaseproof paper, tucking it under the tin to secure. You need to have the tension of the paper just right so that it protects the cake from drying out without dipping down onto the surface and sticking to it.

Bake for 25–30 minutes until risen and golden and a skewer inserted comes out clean.

While the cake is baking, heat the lemon juice and sugar together in a small heavy- bottomed saucepan, stirring frequently until the sugar has dissolved. Put aside to cool.

When the cake is ready, leave it in its tin, prick the surface lightly with a wooden cocktail stick or a fork and spoon the drizzle evenly all over the top. Keep the cake in the tin until it is completely cold and the drizzle has soaked in. Cut into squares and store in an airtight tin.

MARMALADE SQUARES

*This is quite a versatile recipe. It makes a lovely sponge pudding fresh from the oven with custard. As a cake, you can drizzle it with orange glacé icing or eat it plain: alternatively, spread with a little butter (fantastic with a cup of tea for a quick emergency breakfast). It's also good with lemon zest instead of orange, and the squares work well as part of a mixed plate of cakes with **Slightly Restrained Elevenses Brownie** (see page 165).*

You will need a greased 20cm (8in) square brownie tin

Preheat oven to 160ºC (fan oven) or equivalent.

Whiz the butter, sugar and marmalade together until combined and fluffy. Sieve about a tablespoon of flour over the top and add the eggs. Whiz briefly until mixed. Sieve in the rest of the flour and add the orange zest. Whiz briefly and add the warm water. Whiz until everything is mixed together but not over mixed.

Pour into the prepared tin and bake for approximately 25-30 minutes or until risen and golden and a skewer inserted comes out clean.

Leave in the tin for a while then cut into squares and finish cooling on a wire rack. Store in an airtight tin when cold. If you are eating it as a pudding, serve immediately with custard.

110g (4oz) butter, softened
50g (2oz) unrefined caster sugar
2 tablespoons marmalade (a fairly light one with thin slivers of peel works well)
175g (6oz) self-raising flour
2 eggs
Finely grated zest of 1 orange
2 tablespoons warm water

Sieve the icing sugar into a bowl and stir in the juice. Beat with a wooden spoon until smooth and glossy. Drizzle diagonal lines of icing across the cake before you cut it into squares. You can use a piping bag for this but you can equally well let it drip off a tablespoon.

Optional orange glacé icing
50g (2oz) icing sugar
Approximately 1 tablespoon fresh orange juice

GINGERBREAD

You will have great fun making this: it's like mixing up an edible mud pie and it smells gorgeous as it comes out of the oven. This is quite an extreme-tasting version for lovers of seriously dark gingerbread but instructions for a lighter-flavoured version are included below.

110g (4oz) butter	You will need a greased 20cm (8in) square brownie tin
4 generous tablespoons black treacle	Preheat oven to 150ºC (fan oven) or equivalent.
50g (2oz) unrefined caster sugar	Melt the butter, treacle, sugar and water in a small heavy-bottomed saucepan, over a moderate heat, stirring constantly. Once it has melted and the mixture is smooth, pour it into a large bowl and set aside to cool.
4 tablespoons water	
110g (4oz) plain flour	Once it is cool, sieve the flour, bicarbonate of soda and spices over the top and stir in the eggs and the ground almonds. Mix everything together thoroughly and pour into the prepared tin. Bake for 30–40 minutes or until the top is springy to the touch and a skewer inserted comes out clean. If your oven is very fierce, check after 30 minutes: the finished gingerbread should be lovely and moist with a slightly fluffy texture. Leave to settle in the tin for a few minutes, then turn out and cool on a wire rack: if your tin is non-stick, use one of those fairly heavy-duty plastic serrated picnic knives to loosen the edges. Cut into squares.
1 teaspoon bicarbonate of soda	
1–2 teaspoons mixed spice	
2–3 teaspoons ground ginger	
2 eggs, lightly beaten	This makes a very nice and sustaining lunchtime snack with some thin slices of cheese and a crisp apple. Black treacle, incidentally, contains useful amounts of iron. After a couple of days, you may like to spread the gingerbread with a little butter.
110g (4oz) ground almonds	

To make a lighter gingerbread
You might prefer this lighter version. If so, use 2 tablespoons of golden syrup and 2 tablespoons of black treacle, and 2oz of dark brown sugar instead of unrefined caster sugar. This is because for the darker version you need more sweetness, and for the lighter version with the golden syrup, you need less sweetness and more flavour.

To make gingerbread with sultanas
Either version of this gingerbread is also good with a few sultanas scattered through it: not too many, 50g (2oz) is just about right. Add to the mixture with the flour. If you would prefer them plumped up a bit, add them to the butter and treacle mixture once it has started to melt. They add an extra hint of sweetness and moisture.

SLIGHTLY RESTRAINED ELEVENSES BROWNIE

This is not a super-duper luxury brownie oozing with fabulously rich chocolate; it is more of a restrained affair suitable for a treat with a cup of coffee or tea. It is also popular with children. Some brownies can be a bit tooth-achingly sweet: this recipe makes a less sweet, less rich brownie with a lovely deep chocolatey flavour. Having said all this, these brownies are not exactly a diet food, so don't go too mad!

You will need a greased 20cm (8in) square brownie tin

Preheat oven to 180ºC (fan oven) or equivalent.

Whiz the softened butter and sugar together until combined and fluffy. Sieve in a little flour and add the eggs. Add the rest of the flour, the cocoa powder, the ground almonds and milk. Whiz until smooth, stopping a couple of times to scrape the mixture down from the sides.

Remove the blade and scrape into the prepared tin, easing it into the corners.

Bake for approximately 25 minutes; depending on your oven it could be a fraction less or a little more. A skewer inserted should *just* show very slight traces of mixture.

Mark into squares and cool in the tin: if you are worried about scratching your tin, use a sturdy plastic picnic knife. Cover with a clean tea towel to keep the brownies moist as they cool. Store in an airtight tin when completely cold.

175g (6oz) butter, softened
175g (6oz) unrefined
  caster sugar
75g (3oz) self-raising flour
3 eggs, lightly beaten
25g (1oz) good-quality
  cocoa powder
50g (2oz) ground almonds
2 tablespoons milk

FLAPJACKS

Flapjacks are a much-loved favourite with most people. A square is a sustaining addition to a child's lunch box.

110g (4oz) butter
110g (4oz) demerara sugar
2 tablespoons golden syrup
2 tablespoons water
½ teaspoon salt
1 teaspoon good-quality vanilla extract
225g (8oz) rolled oats

You will need a greased 20cm (8in) square brownie tin

Preheat oven to 160ºC (fan oven) or equivalent.

Put the butter, sugar, syrup and water into something like a wok-style frying pan over a moderate heat until the butter and syrup have melted and all the sugar has dissolved and lost its grittiness. Stir in the salt and vanilla and then add the oats a few at a time, stirring as you go so that all the oats are completely coated. Press into the prepared tin, smoothing the top firmly and evenly with the back of a wet tablespoon. You may need to re-wet the spoon a couple of times. Bake for 20–30 minutes or until pale golden. Remove from the oven and leave for 10 minutes or so to settle and firm up. Mark into squares (or triangles or bars, if you prefer) and leave in the tin until completely cold. Store in an airtight tin.

You may like to use a sturdy plastic picnic knife to mark the squares so as not to damage your baking tin.

Raisin Flapjacks
Add 50g (2oz) raisins to the mixture. If you would like the raisins plumped up a bit, add them to the butter and sugar mixture as it melts.

Apricot Flapjacks
Add 50–110g (2–4oz) of the moister, ready-to-eat type dried apricots, each one cut into roughly 6 pieces, to the mixture with the oats.

✓ **Useful Note** Be careful when pressing the Raisin and Apricot Flapjacks into the tin that you don't have any exposed fruit sticking up out of the mixture: the heat of the oven will bake it too hard to eat.

SCONES

There is something in the British psyche that loves scones. Scones conjure up all kinds of happy pictures – hot buttered scones in the winter, cream teas on summer holidays (or any time at all really!) – and they are always a welcome treat.

It is really easy to make them at home but it's also easy to convince yourself that you can't. This may be because they can end up flat or hard and tough or have that bitter tang on the tongue of too much bicarbonate of soda. The scones from the re-rolled trimmings are never quite as good as the first ones so try to minimise re-rolling if you can. You could use a square cutter and this would certainly minimise re-rolling but somehow a square scone is *just all wrong*!

If the weather is very hot and heavy you may find your dough is a bit sloppier and stickier than normal and maybe even a bit 'curdled' looking. This makes the dough more difficult to work with but the finished scones will still taste good.

How to be sure of scone success
- Try not to over-handle the dough, this makes them tough;
- Roll the dough out quite thickly – a good three quarters of an inch or a generous couple of centimetres – otherwise you will have a flat biscuit;
- Warm the milk to lukewarm to help them rise well;
- Don't overcook or they will be hard;
- Use two parts of cream of tartar to one of bicarbonate of soda; this will help them rise beautifully, give an extra fluffy texture and avoid any possibility of the bitter tang mentioned above.

Preheat oven to 200ºC (fan oven) or equivalent.

Sieve the flour, bicarbonate of soda and cream of tartar into a bowl large enough to give you room to manoeuvre, rub in the softened butter, stir in the sugar and fruit, if using. Mix the milk in gradually; an ordinary dinner knife works well.

Knead gently and place on a floured board. Roll out quite thickly (see above), with a floured rolling pin, and cut out with a 6cm (2½in) cutter; a fluted one looks professional. Re-roll the trimmings and cut out again.

Bake on a greased baking sheet for 8–10 minutes until well risen and golden brown on top. Cool on a wire rack. Eat with butter or strawberry jam and clotted cream.

MAKES about 8–9 scones (if you want to make more, make separate batches, rather than one big one; it's easier to handle)

225g (8oz) plain flour
1 teaspoon bicarbonate of soda
2 teaspoons cream of tartar
40g (1½oz) softened butter
25g (1oz) unrefined caster sugar
150ml (¼ pint) semi-skimmed milk, warmed slightly

For fruit scones, add 75g (3oz) of raisins or sultanas or a mixture

Freezing

These are best when completely fresh but you can freeze them: allow the scones to cool completely, put them in a freezer bag, secure the top and store in the freezer.

A note on jam

The quality of the jam is just as important as the scones and cream for a really good cream tea. Strawberry jam is the most traditional choice and a few sliced strawberries on the side as well adds up to cream tea heaven.

WELSH CAKES

These are best eaten straight away while warm but they are still nice the next day in lunch boxes. They are handy for picnics too. Eat on their own or with butter or thin slices of cheese.

MAKES approximately 28

225g (8oz) plain flour
½ teaspoon baking powder
50g (2oz) butter
50g (2oz) block vegetable shortening or lard
50g (2oz) unrefined granulated sugar
75g (3oz) currants or raisins or sultanas, or a mixture
1 egg, beaten
3 tablespoons milk
Butter or oil to grease the pan: butter gives the best flavour

Sieve the flour and baking powder into a large mixing bowl and rub in the butter and shortening. Stir in the sugar and dried fruit. Beat the egg separately and mix with the milk. Stir into the mixture to make a stiff dough: a dinner knife is the best tool for this.

Once the liquid is all stirred in, it will still be fairly crumbly so bring it together with your hands: flour them first. Roll out onto a floured board to just over ½cm thick – this is quite crucial: too thick and they won't cook through properly, too thin and they'll be too crisp. Cut into rounds with a 6cm (2½in) cutter; a fluted one looks best.

Once you have cut out all the cakes, grease a frying pan: it's quite handy to have two frying pans on the go; that way you can cook them all more quickly. Get the pan(s) to a nice even, moderate heat.

Cook the Welsh Cakes, a few at a time, for a few minutes, turning a couple of times. Don't go off and leave them or get distracted! Once they are cooking nicely, you'll hear them 'singing' to you: just like the very similar 'Singing Hinnies' they make in the north of England. You'll know when they are ready as they'll be a nice golden brown on each side.

Sprinkle with a little caster sugar just before serving, if you like, or leave them just as they are. Store any left over in an airtight tin.

Useful Note The pan must be hot enough or the cakes will be greasy. Don't overload the pan as you need to give yourself room to turn them over. Take care not to turn them over too soon as they are quite delicate at this stage, and be careful not to burn them, particularly with the last batch, when the pan may start to overheat. All this sounds a bit of a fiddle but they are easy really; very quick and well worth making the effort to get them right.

ALL KINDS OF CRISPY CAKES

Crispy Cakes are so easy to make: just a bit of melting and stirring. The fiddliest part is spooning them into the paper cases. Most children love Crispy Cakes – and adults too: if you make them smaller and put them into petits fours cases you can call them 'clusters' instead and serve them with coffee.

The two main types of Crispy Cake are the ones made from chocolate and the ones made with butter and sugar and syrup. These can be further subdivided into those made with cornflakes and those made with crispy rice cereal, different kinds of chocolate, and those with extras such as dried fruit and nuts. Crispy Cakes are a great starting point (if a bit messy) for cooking with children. If you are using crispy rice cereal try to get the unsweetened kind or the cakes will be very sweet. Rice cereal tends to make the coating stretch a bit further.

GOLDEN SYRUP CRISPY CAKES

These are lovely and simple: you can make them with either cornflakes or crispy rice cereal. If you are making these for tiny tots, rice cereal is usually easier and kinder for them to eat as cornflakes can be a bit sharp and 'poky' for little mouths, as anyone who has been stabbed in the roof of the mouth with an upright cornflake will tell you.

You need both the sugar and the syrup as the sugar helps with the setting and the syrup with the coating. Similarly, butter sets better and has a much nicer flavour than margarine. Finally, yummy as these are, they are probably best kept for an occasional treat as they are a bit stickier on the teeth than the chocolate ones.

ORIGINAL GOLDEN SYRUP CRISPY CAKES

MAKES approximately 12

25g (1oz) butter
25g (1oz) unrefined caster
sugar (use granulated in
an emergency but it will
take longer to dissolve)
1 tablespoon golden syrup
50g (2oz) cornflakes or
unsweetened crispy rice
cereal

You will need paper cake cases and a 12-cup muffin or tart tin will be helpful

Melt the butter, sugar and syrup together in a heavy-bottomed saucepan until the sugar has dissolved and it is bubbling. Let it bubble for a few moments, stirring all the time to get a bit of a toffee reaction going, but don't overdo it or the cakes will be jaw-breakingly hard. Pour into a roomy bowl and stir in the cereal gently with a wooden spoon. If you are using cornflakes, crush them slightly through your fingers to soften the sharp edges.

Although you won't be baking these, it makes things a lot easier if you actually set your paper cases out in a muffin or tart tin. The cakes keep their shape better and it's easier to fill the cases. Fill each case, using two teaspoons to help you, and leave them to set for a couple of hours, more if possible. Store in an airtight tin.

If you want to double up on quantity, make two separate batches rather than one large one. This is because if you try to do them all at once the mixture will have started to set before you have got it all into the cases.

PUFFED WHEAT CRISPY CAKES

Although this is made with puffed wheat it tastes deliciously like the popcorn you can buy at the cinema. Make in the same way as the previous recipe.

MAKES approximately
12–14

25g (1oz) butter
25g (1oz) unrefined caster sugar
1 tablespoon golden syrup
50g (2oz) unsweetened puffed wheat cereal

NUTTY CLUSTERS

The two kinds of cereal and the nuts work well together. Follow the procedure for the previous recipes. These are great in petits fours cases.

MAKES approximately
10–12 cakes, double for petits fours cases

25g (1oz) butter
25g (1oz) unrefined caster sugar
1 tablespoon golden syrup
40g (1½ oz) combined crispy rice cereal and slightly crushed cornflakes
25g (1oz) mixed chopped nuts

Chocolate Crispy Cakes

The only slightly tricky part here is dealing with melting chocolate: if you go too far the chocolate will become grainy and it's not really edible at that point. You can melt your chocolate perfectly well in a bowl over the top of a pan of hot water but it's a lot easier in short bursts in the microwave. It is *very difficult* to over-melt it using this method. Add the cereal to the melted chocolate rather than the other way round: if you try to pour the chocolate over the cereal you will cool it down too quickly and some will stay stuck to the pouring bowl.

Milk Chocolate Crispy Cakes

These are the classic chocolate crispy cakes.

MAKES approximately 10	You will need paper cake cases and a muffin or tart tin will be helpful
100g good-quality milk chocolate 40g (1½oz) butter 50g (2oz) slightly crushed cornflakes (or crispy rice cereal)	Break up the chocolate and put it in a heatproof bowl. Melt it in the microwave on High, in 30-second blasts, stirring in between. It should take roughly 2 to 2½ minutes altogether. Cut the butter into small pieces and add to the melted chocolate. Give it a good stir: it should melt of its own accord in the warmed chocolate. Working quickly, stir in the cornflakes or rice cereal with a metal spoon, making sure everything is completely coated. Use two teaspoons to divide the mixture between the cake cases. Leave to set in a cool, dry place for a couple of hours, more if possible. Store in an airtight tin when cold.

MILK CHOCOLATE AND RAISIN CRISPY CAKES

You will need paper cake cases and a muffin or tart tin will be helpful

Make as for previous recipe.

MAKES approximately 10

100g good-quality milk
    chocolate
40g (1½oz) butter
40g (1½oz) slightly crushed
    cornflakes (or crispy
    rice cereal)
25g (1oz) raisins

HALF MILK, HALF DARK CHOCOLATE CRISPY CAKES

Either of the previous recipes works well made with half milk and half dark chocolate melted together.

DARK CHOCOLATE CRISPY CAKES WITH FRUIT AND NUTS AND SEEDS

No precise quantities are given here and no butter is added. These appeal more to older children and adults.

You can make up your own combination: a mixture of rice cereal and slightly crushed cornflakes, a few seeds, some chopped nuts and some dried fruit of your choice.

Melt the chocolate as before, and stir in small amounts of your chosen bits and pieces. Try to work fairly quickly before the chocolate starts to set and don't try to pack too much in: you need a certain amount of 'free chocolate' to stick everything together. Spoon fairly smartly into paper cases, and leave to set in a cool place. Store in an airtight tin.

These also work well as 'clusters' in petits fours cases.

100g good-quality dark
    chocolate (you may like
    to double up and use
    200g)
Cornflakes or crispy rice
    cereal
Dried fruit such as raisins,
    cranberries, finely
    chopped apricot
Chopped nuts and, or,
    seeds

SNOWBALLS

Use rice cereal for these as they are slightly easier to mould into an approximate ball shape.

MAKES approximately 12

100g good-quality white
   chocolate
40g (1½oz) crispy rice
   cereal

Melt the chocolate as before and stir in the crispy rice. Using two teaspoons, divide between the paper cases, shaping them as best you can into approximate balls. Leave to cool for a couple of hours, more if possible, and store in an airtight tin.

WHITE CHOCOLATE AND CRANBERRY CRISPY CAKES

White chocolate and cranberries are a scrumptious combination.

MAKES approximately
   10–12

150g good-quality white
   chocolate
50g (2oz) slightly crushed
   cornflakes
25g (1oz) dried
   cranberries

Melt the chocolate as before and stir in the cornflakes and cranberries. Using two teaspoons, divide between the paper cases. Leave to cool for a couple of hours, more if possible, and store in an airtight tin.

These also work well as 'clusters' in petits fours cases.

EASTER NESTS

You can't have a section on crispy cakes without featuring their close relation: the Easter Nest. These are a much-loved Easter tradition in many households. It goes without saying that children will be heavily involved in their production. As well as the sugar-coated eggs, you may like to include some fluffy yellow Easter chicks once the chocolate has set.

Break up the shredded wheat in a bowl (try to keep as many long wheaty strands as possible, if you can, and not crush it all too much).

Break up the chocolate and put it in a heatproof bowl. Melt it on High, in 30-second blasts, stirring in between. It should take roughly 2–2½ minutes altogether. Cut the butter into small pieces and add to the melted chocolate. Give it a good stir; it should melt of its own accord in the warmth from the chocolate.

Add the shredded wheat to the melted chocolate mixture, a little at a time, stirring it all together with a metal spoon as quickly as you can before it starts to set too much.

Spoon into the cake cases, then go back and make a dip with the back of a teaspoon in each one (it helps if the spoon is slightly wet, but not dripping, so keep a jug of water standing by and keep an eye on things). Leave to cool for a couple of hours, more if possible.

The eggs
If you would like the eggs to stick to the nests slightly, arrange them in the nests before the chocolate has set. In practice though, this can lead to a lot of very smeared eggs and squashed nests. It is easier to put them in the nests once the chocolate has set, even if they do keep rolling out again.

MAKES approximately 10

50g (2oz) shredded wheat
    cereal (this usually
    equates to 2 biscuits)
100g good-quality milk
    chocolate
40g (1½oz) butter
Coloured, sugar-coated
    speckled 'mini eggs'

You will need a tart or
    muffin tin or two and
    some paper cake cases

SUMMER HAYSTACKS

This is a summer holiday version of the Easter Nest, but a bit simpler. The haystacks contain a little more chocolate, proportionally, than the nests.

MAKES approximately 8

150g good-quality white chocolate
50g (2oz) shredded wheat

You will need a tart or muffin tin and some paper cake cases

Break up the shredded wheat in a bowl (try to keep as many long wheaty strands as possible, if you can, and not crush it all too much).

Melt the chocolate as before. Add the shredded wheat to the melted chocolate mixture, a little at a time, stirring it all together with a metal spoon as quickly as you can before it starts to set too much.

Pile the chocolate shredded wheat into the cake cases to resemble (very rough) haystack shapes. Leave to cool for a couple of hours and store in an airtight tin.

CHRISTMAS CAKE

This is a slightly unusual Christmas cake in that you make it using the old-fashioned boiled fruit cake method. This means that the fruit is all beautifully plump and moist so even if you don't get round to making it until just before Christmas it will still taste exactly right. If you like nuts in your Christmas cake add 50g (2oz) of chopped walnuts or mixed nuts at the end, with the flour and eggs. If you prefer to leave out the brandy, just add an extra 30ml (1fl oz) of water instead.

Preheat oven to 150°C (fan oven) or equivalent.

Grease and line a 23cm (9in) loose-bottomed cake tin.

Put all the raisins, currants and sultanas (and dried cherries if you are using them) into a large saucepan with the butter, sugar, spices and water. Bring it all to the boil and simmer gently for five minutes. Leave to cool. Stir in the brandy. At this stage, you can cover the mixture and leave it overnight or you can press on to the next stage.

Cut the glacé cherries, if you are using them, into quarters and dust in a little of the flour. Sieve the rest of the flour into the mixture with the eggs. Stir in the floured cherries and candied peel. Stir everything together thoroughly.

Pour the mixture into the prepared tin and tuck a piece of greaseproof paper loosely round it. Bake for 1¼ hours until it is firm to the touch and a skewer inserted comes out clean.

Leave to cool in the tin slightly before turning out onto a wire rack to cool completely.

When cold, wrap in clean greaseproof paper and store in a tin until ready to ice, just before Christmas.

175g (6oz) raisins
175g (6oz) currants
175g (6oz) sultanas
50g (2oz) glacé or dried
   sour cherries
175g (6oz) butter
250g (8oz) soft dark
   brown sugar
½ teaspoon each of
   cinnamon, ground ginger
   and mixed spice
210ml (7fl oz) water
30ml (1fl oz) brandy
275g (10oz) self-raising
   flour
3 very fresh eggs, beaten
50g (2oz) candied peel,
   finely sliced and cut into
   small pieces

ICING THE CAKE

A few days before Christmas cover the cake with marzipan and, if you have time, leave it to dry out slightly for a couple of days before icing. You will need to cover the cake with apricot or marmalade glaze before you put on the marzipan. You can buy ready-made marzipan and roll-on icing but it is really easy to make the marzipan and icing yourself, and they then become elements of the cake that taste lovely in their own right. You have something you actually want to eat rather than just a bit of decoration.

Apricot or Marmalade Glaze

This works as a kind of fruity glue and helps to stick the almond paste to the cake. Warm 2 tablespoons of apricot jam or marmalade (you will need to remove any shreds of peel) until it becomes slightly runny. Brush over the top and sides of your cake with a pastry brush if you have one. If not, use a dessertspoon to spoon it over the top of the cake and then use the back of the spoon to smooth it down and over the sides.

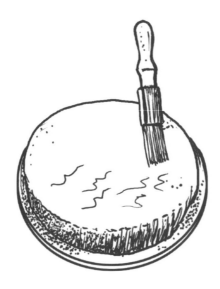

HOME-MADE ALMOND PASTE OR MARZIPAN

Almond paste is very simple to make at home and tastes quite different from the bought version: it's fresh and almondy and not at all cloying. You can make this by hand but it's easier with a food processor.

Sieve the icing sugar into a bowl and stir in the ground almonds. Tip carefully into the bowl of your food processor. Add the egg yolk, almond extract and lemon juice. Whiz for a few seconds and then stop and scrape the mixture from around the sides into the centre and whiz again. Repeat this a few times. The *second* the mixture congregates together on the side of the bowl, stop whizzing *immediately*! If you carry on it will become oily and over-processed. Take the mixture out of the processor, gathering up any loose crumbs, and put it onto a large board or worktop dusted with icing sugar. Knead it gently for a few seconds and then roll it into a ball, dusting with more icing sugar as necessary. Dust your rolling pin with icing sugar and carefully roll the almond paste flat until it is large enough in circumference to cover the whole surface area of your cake, including the top and the sides. Lift it carefully onto the glazed cake. You might find it easier to lift it by rolling it round your rolling pin and then unrolling it again over the cake. Using both hands, gently and carefully smooth and shape it round the cake and trim the extra from around the bottom of the cake with a knife. Sieve a little more icing sugar over the top and smooth it gently with your rolling pin: if you happen to have a child's rolling pin it will make this bit much easier. Wrap in clean greaseproof paper and keep in a cool dry place for a couple of days before icing.

This is sufficient to cover a 23cm (9in) round cake

110g (4oz) icing sugar
225g (8oz) ground almonds
1 very fresh egg yolk
¼–½ teaspoon of natural almond extract
3 tablespoons lemon juice

Separating the egg

Since this isn't going to be cooked, use an egg separator to separate the egg. Alternatively, use two dessertspoons to lift the yolk away from the white, or try **the egg cup trick**: this involves cracking the egg on a small plate or saucer, holding an egg cup upside down over the yolk, and pouring off the white.

CHRISTMAS CAKE ICING

If you like to eat a bit of icing with your cake you may have found the ready-roll fondant type icing can be a bit cloying. The more traditional royal icing can go rock hard after a couple of days and you can be in danger of breaking your teeth. A fairly stiff glacé icing made with lemon juice is a lot easier on the teeth and tastes good too.

If you aren't very good at fancy icing, don't worry: make 'rough icing' instead. With this you don't do any piping at all, but just pile the icing on, rough it up a bit, and pretend the top of the Christmas Cake is a snow scene. The benefits of this are: it's quick and easy, children can have fun helping and you can use all your favourite decorations.

This is sufficient to cover a 23cm (9in) round cake

225g (8oz) icing sugar
Approximately 4 tablespoons lemon juice, sieved through a tea strainer

You will need large a palette knife or a flexible 30cm (12in) ruler

Sieve the icing sugar into a large bowl. Make a well in the middle and pour in the lemon juice. Using a wooden spoon gradually stir the juice into the icing sugar until it is all mixed in: this takes longer than you think, but keep at it. When it is all mixed in keep stirring until it is smooth and glossy. It should be fairly stiff but still pourable.

Try icing the cake on a large dinner plate, turned upside down. You can leave it there until the icing has set and it is then relatively easy to lift it onto its serving plate, using a couple of fish slices. This saves getting everything too messy.

Pour the icing on top of your cake a little at a time and help it gently over the top and sides with the back of a tablespoon; it helps if the spoon is wet so have a jug of water to hand.

Once the cake is covered, smooth it gently with the palette knife or flexible ruler. If you do want to make a snow scene, allow the icing to set slightly and then rough up the surface gently with the back of a spoon to simulate drifts of snow. If you like, you can make a path across the middle (this may take several attempts) and arrange your decorations on either side of the path. At this stage, it's quite difficult to manoeuvre the cake into a tin, so cover with a large cake dome or inverted mixing bowl or cover loosely with foil.

BOILED FRUIT CAKE

The Christmas cake recipe, above, can also be used to make a beautiful moist fruit cake at any time of year. Just leave out the brandy and increase the water by 30ml (1fl oz) instead. Leave out the cherries and candied peel and you may want to consider cutting down the spice to ½ teaspoon of mixed spice, or even leaving out the spice altogether.

PASTRY

Here is a selection of simple homely pastry recipes: some savoury and some sweet. They are all shortcrust but with some slightly different versions. There is a simple, straightforward one using plain flour, butter and shortening; and a sweet, all-butter pastry. There is also a pasty pastry that uses strong bread flour, and a sweet version of this as well.

It's really easy to make pastry in the food processor; be aware, though, that you can actually over-process it so take care. You can process it until it forms a ball, then you must stop the machine immediately. Usually, it's best to whiz the pastry mix until it starts to clump together and take it out before the ball stage, then finish kneading it gently together in your hands. It makes the pastry a little lighter and more crumbly in texture. A 175g (6oz) mix is usually the most that the average food processor can cope with at one time, so if you are making more, do it in batches of 110 or 175g (4 or 6oz).

Oven temperatures

Please be aware that individual oven performance can vary tremendously. An average temperature of 180ºC or equivalent has been suggested for most recipes in this section. Some ovens may need to be set higher – 200ºC or equivalent – some may need to be set lower.

PASTIES (CORNISH STYLE)

Many Cornish people make pasty pastry with strong bread flour, and it works brilliantly: it makes a very slightly flaky and more elastic dough, handy for easing over the bumpy filling. It is also crucial to slice the steak and vegetables thinly, as you need them to cook through completely in the time it takes the pastry to cook. The pieces should be fairly small otherwise they will poke through the raw pastry and tear it. Also, don't put a slit in the pasty because part of the cooking process is done through the steam that is generated inside the pasty.

The traditional cuts of beef for a pasty are chuck, blade or skirt: your local butcher will be able to advise you. If you are making a cheese pasty, slice the vegetables thinly in the same way but dice the cheese: if you grate it or slice it too finely, it will overcook and start to seep out. If you are making your pastry in the processor and want to double the quantity, make it in two batches so the processor can cope and mix it properly.

STEAK PASTY

Preheat oven to 180ºC (fan oven) or equivalent.

Put the flour, fats and salt into the bowl of your processor and whiz into crumbs. Add the water and whiz until it starts to come together but is still crumbly. Put it onto a floured board and knead gently into a ball. Let it rest while you prepare the filling.

Peel and slice the vegetables to a thickness of between 1–2mm (about ⅛in). Cut them across into pieces not much larger than a centimetre (about ½in). Slice the steak in the same way.

Roll out the pastry and cut into circles using a plate or cereal bowl to guide you. Lay the circles onto the baking tray. Put your filling in the middle, seasoning with plenty of pepper and a little salt as you go. Brush the edges of the pastry with water.

Gather the pastry from the sides and bring them together at the top, gently pressing them together as you go. This will give you the characteristic wavy 'crimp'. Brush with beaten egg for a glossy, professional finish and bake for 20–25 minutes or until golden brown.

Pasties can be 'crimped' at the top or the side. You might find the 'top crimp' easier to manage.

MAKES 2 pasties or 3 smaller ones

175g (6oz) strong bread flour
40g (1½oz) butter, diced
40g (1½oz) block vegetable shortening, diced
½ teaspoon salt
3 tablespoons cold water
1 smallish onion
1 smallish potato
A piece of swede (or a small carrot in an emergency!), slightly smaller than the potato
110g (4oz) chuck or blade or skirt steak
Plenty of freshly ground black pepper and a touch of salt
Beaten egg to glaze

You will need a greased baking tray

CHEESE AND ONION PASTY

MAKES 2 pasties or 3 smaller ones

1 small onion
1 smallish potato
25–50g (1–2oz) Cheddar cheese
Plenty of freshly ground black pepper

Pastry, as before

Preheat oven to 180ºC (fan oven) or equivalent.

Make your pastry and proceed as for the Steak Pasty above. The potato and onion should be sliced thinly, as before; the cheese should be diced into roughly 1cm cubes.

A word of caution before you tuck in

If you are going to eat your pasty hot, cut into it first and wait a few moments for the steam to escape, otherwise you could give yourself a nasty burn!

STEAK AND POTATO PIE

This is a great heartening pie for a winter weekend lunch or supper. You will need one of those old-fashioned pie funnels to stop the pastry from falling into the filling.

SERVES 4

For the filling
450g (1lb) potatoes
450g (1lb) braising steak, or preferably feather steak (ask your local butcher)
1 tablespoon plain flour
Oil for frying
1 fair-sized onion
1 tablespoon Worcestershire sauce
1 teaspoon black treacle
Freshly ground black or white pepper
¼ teaspoon salt, or to taste

To make the filling
Peel the potatoes, cut into quarters and boil in unsalted water until just tender. Drain and set aside to cool, but keep the cooking water.

Cut the steak into bite-sized pieces, and coat in the flour. Heat the oil in a pan and fry the onion. Remove from the pan and keep warm, check there is enough oil left in the pan and fry the meat, turning frequently until it is lightly browned. Return the onion to the pan. Put the Worcestershire sauce and black treacle into about 275ml (½ pint) of the cooking water from the potatoes, and add to the pan, season with pepper.

Stir it all together and bring to the boil, stirring frequently. Leave it to simmer gently, stirring from time to time, until the meat is tender and the gravy has thickened. Top up with more potato water if necessary. Check for seasoning and add any salt towards the end. Meanwhile, make the pastry.

To make the pastry

You may find this easier in a food processor. Put the fats, flour and salt into the bowl of your food processor. Whiz until it forms crumbs. Add the water and whiz until the mixture starts to clump together but is still crumbly.

Remove from the machine, put onto a floured work surface and knead gently into a ball. Flour your rolling pin and roll the dough to a thickness of slightly less than ½cm. Put your pie dish upside down onto the pastry and cut round it so you have a piece of pastry slightly larger than your dish.

Grease the rim of the dish. Using the leftover pastry, cut some strips the right width and press gently all round the rim. Use your rolling pin to firm it gently. Put the filling into the dish with enough gravy to cover. Reserve the rest of the gravy. Put your pie funnel into the centre of the pie filling. Slice your cooked potatoes and arrange in a thick layer over the top.

Brush the pastry rim with water. Lift your pastry lid into position on the pie. Ease the pastry down over the funnel so it shows through. Press the edges down gently. Finally, brush the top with beaten egg and bake in a preheated oven at 180ºC (fan oven) or equivalent for about 20 minutes or until the pastry is golden brown.

Serve with the leftover gravy and steamed vegetables.

For the pastry

40g (1½oz) cold butter, diced

40g (1½oz) cold block vegetable shortening, diced

175g (6 oz) strong bread flour (as used in Cornwall for the best pasty pastry)

¼ teaspoon salt

3 tablespoons cold water

Beaten egg to glaze

You will need a 1¼ litre (2 pint) pie dish with a flat rim, and a pie funnel

SAVOURY FLANS

Baking blind

I fought shy of baking pastry cases blind for a long time, thinking it was too complicated or too much trouble or something. Needless to say, my flans had soggy bottoms and the sides fell in. Then one day I just put the loose bottom of my flan tin onto some greaseproof paper, drew round it, cut it out and put it in my pastry case. I filled it to the top with dried peas and put it in the oven for 20 minutes. It came out perfect.

How hard was that? I realised then that preventing a soggy bottom is only half the story: if you fill the case nearly to the top it stops the sides falling in as well. Also, ideally you should be baking your pastry at a higher temperature than you need for a delicate quiche type filling of cream and eggs, so once you have cooked your flan case, you can lower the temperature for the filling.

You can use any dried pulses to bake blind or you can buy special ceramic baking beans. The ceramic ones work much better: they conduct the heat to the surfaces of the pastry more efficiently and last indefinitely.

CHEESE AND ONION FLAN

This is really what we now call quiche, but having read a definition years ago of genuine Quiche Lorraine, I haven't the nerve to call this recipe quiche! The genuine article contains only cream, eggs and bacon, no cheese and no onion. Never mind, whatever it's called it tastes lovely!

For the pastry	To make the pastry
175g (6oz) plain flour	Preheat the oven to 190ºC (fan oven) or equivalent.
40g (1½oz) butter, cold and cut into small pieces	
40g (1½oz) vegetable shortening, cold and cut into small pieces	Sieve the flour carefully into the bowl of your food processor and add the butter, vegetable shortening and salt. Whiz into fine crumbs. Add the water and whiz again. Once it is starting to form big crumbs and clump together, turn it out onto a lightly floured board and knead it gently into a ball.
Pinch of salt	
2–3 tablespoons cold water	
	Try to keep it round and roll it gently with a lightly floured rolling pin into a large disc of roughly ½cm (¼in) thick. Roll it round your rolling pin and manoeuvre it gently off the rolling pin and on top of the prepared flan tin. Hold the sides upright as best you can while you settle it into the bottom of the tin, firming gently with your fingers. Trim away the excess. Prick the bottom lightly all over with a fork.

Put a circle of greaseproof paper on the bottom of the pastry case and fill it nearly to the top with baking beans (see above). Bake for 15–20 minutes until pale golden (but not dark brown). Leave to settle for a few moments and remove the beans from the pastry case (tip them out very gently into something like a fairly wide metal colander until they cool down, taking care not to damage the edge of the pastry).

✓ **Useful Note** If your flan tin is the fluted metal type with a sharp top edge, simply pass your rolling pin over the top when you want to trim off the excess pastry and it will just fall away.

To make the filling
Reduce the oven to 160ºC (fan oven) or equivalent.

Peel and slice the onion fairly finely. Fry until soft and barely coloured. Drain on kitchen paper. Grate the cheese.

Beat the egg and egg yolk gently together with the mustard powder (stir it through a tea strainer with a teaspoon to prevent it clumping together) and pepper. Add the cream and whisk in lightly.

Spread the onion evenly over the bottom of the pastry case and pour the cream and egg mixture over the top. Finally, scatter the cheese evenly over the surface. Bake for 15 minutes or until risen and golden. Serve warm or cold.

✓ **Useful Note** If you find yourself with a few odds and ends of Cheddar type cheese cluttering up the fridge, run them through the food processor until they are roughly grated. Store in the freezer, in a freezer bag or box. You can use this straight from the freezer.

For the filling
1 small onion and a little oil
50–75g (2–3oz) well-flavoured Cheddar cheese
1 egg
1 egg yolk
Pinch dry mustard powder
Freshly ground black or white pepper
6 tablespoons cream (single or double, but preferably not extra thick)

You will need a greased 20cm (8in) loose-bottomed flan tin

CHEESE AND BACON FLAN

Make the flan exactly as above but also fry 2 or 3 rashers of lean bacon, cut into small squares or matchsticks: add a little oil to the pan if necessary. The bacon should be cooked through but not crisp. Drain on kitchen paper and scatter over the base of the flan with the onion.

 Useful Note You can cut the bacon with sharp kitchen scissors straight into the frying pan.

LITTLE CHEESE FLANS

These are a bit of a fiddle to make but they are so delicious it's worth it. They are great for picnics and parties. There is no need to bake blind: as they are so small the filling and pastry can cook together.

MAKES about 16	Preheat oven to 180ºC (fan oven) or equivalent.
You will need a greased 12-cup tart tin and a 7½cm (3in) plain cutter	Make up 175g (6oz) pastry as above and the same quantity of your chosen filling. Cut out the pastry rounds and press them gently into the tart tin. (If you have a second tart tin it would be useful, otherwise bake a separate part batch.)

Spoon the filling into the unbaked cases, as above, and bake for around 12–15 minutes or until the pastry is cooked and the filling is risen and golden. Eat warm or cold.

Useful Note If you are making these for a party you can cut out the pastry rounds, line your greased tins, wrap them in a large freezer bag and put them in the freezer. Take them out when they are needed and they should have enough time to defrost while you make the filling. If you don't have enough tins, you can freeze the pastry rounds in stacks, in a freezer bag. Defrost them before you try to put them in the baking tin or they will break.

APPLE PIE AND RELATIONS

Once you have made this really easy pie you will be off at a gallop and able to make apple dumplings, tarts and turnovers as well.

OLD-FASHIONED APPLE PLATE PIE

This is a 'one crust' apple pie, which means it has a pastry lid, but no bottom. You need a Pyrex pie plate to make it in, or something similar. There are several things that make this pastry extra nice. It's made with butter and contains a spoonful of sugar, plus the top is sprinkled with sugar before baking as well. Also, the flour is strong bread flour instead of ordinary plain flour. As with their pasties, Cornish cooks often use this for their home-baked apple pies.

Despite the usual view that strong bread flour is no good for pastry, it works really well in these instances, producing a slightly elastic pastry that smooths happily over bumpy bits of pasty filling or slices of apple. The pastry also has a nice, faintly flaky quality: it doesn't chill well though, so use it straight away, and it doesn't respond well to re-rolling. Finally, instead of cooking apples (such as Bramleys) use dessert apples and a splash of apple juice.

Preheat oven to 180ºC (fan oven) or equivalent.

Cut the butter into dice and put into the bowl of your food processor. Add the flour and salt. Whiz briefly into fine breadcrumbs. Add the sugar and give one quick turn of the processor to mix it in. Add the water and whiz until the mixture starts to clump together but is still crumbly. Remove from the machine, put onto a floured board and knead gently into a ball. Using a floured rolling pin, roll it out to a thickness of a little less than ½cm (¼in).

Put your pie plate on top of the rolled out pastry and cut round it with a knife so that you end up with a circle slightly larger than the plate.

Peel and core the apples and slice them thinly. Arrange them evenly in the pie plate, piling them up slightly in the middle. Add the apple juice.

Grease the rim of the plate and cut some strips from the leftover pastry the width of the rim. Use these strips to line the rim: press them down gently so that they join together; you will probably use about five strips.

Next, brush the pastry rim with water and lift your circle of pastry on top: you might like to use your rolling pin to lift it. Brush the top of the pie with water and sprinkle with caster sugar. Make a neat slit in the top with your knife.

Bake for 20–25 minutes, or until the pie is pale golden brown on top.

Did you ever wonder what the expression 'easy as pie' meant? Now you know!

Quantities given are for an approximately 23cm (9in) pie plate

75g (3oz) butter
175g (6oz) strong bread flour
Pinch of salt
1 tablespoon unrefined caster sugar, plus more for sprinkling
3 tablespoons very cold water
3 dessert apples: Cox's are perfect
1 tablespoon apple juice (or water if no juice available)

RHUBARB PLATE PIE

This is a version of the pie above, made with rhubarb. It is especially good made with lovely deep pink new season rhubarb. Rhubarb makes a lot of juice so it is better to part cook it first so you can drain most of it away. If you don't, juice will bubble and run everywhere and the pastry will be soggy.

Pastry, as for **Old-Fashioned Apple Plate Pie**, above
About 700g (1½lb) rhubarb
75–110g (3–4oz) unrefined granulated sugar
1–2 tablespoons cold water

Preheat oven to 180ºC (fan oven) or equivalent.

Trim the rhubarb and cut into short lengths. Put into a saucepan with 1–2 tablespoons of water and cook gently until it is starting to soften and the juices are running. Remove from the heat and strain off the juice.

Roll out your pastry, as above, and arrange the strained rhubarb in a pie plate. Sprinkle the sugar over it and stir it in lightly. Cover with pastry, using the method above, and brush with water and sprinkle with sugar in the same way. Make a neat slit in the top and bake for 20–25 minutes or until pale golden brown.

Please don't attempt to eat this pie straight out of the oven: the rhubarb will have made more juice and it will be *boiling* hot! Serve warm with generous amounts of custard, cream or Greek yoghurt.

APPLE DUMPLINGS

We had a cookery book at home when I was a little girl with a picture of apple dumplings in it. For some reason, I longed to try them and kept asking my mum to make them. We never actually got round to it in the end but it became a bit of a joke: 'And when are we going to have apple dumplings?'

Anyway, here they are, and very nice they are too (and surprisingly easy, after all!). The original recipe called for Bramley apples filled with brown sugar but these are made with dessert apples filled with raisins. The pastry is the same as for the Apple Pie recipe, above: it holds together really well and bakes beautifully.

If you are feeling artistic, you can make some leaves out of the leftover pastry and stick them on, like the ones in my Mum's book.

Preheat oven to 180ºC (fan oven) or equivalent.

Make your pastry as in the apple pie recipe previously. You should be able to fit a 175g (6oz) mix into most food processors.

Peel and core the apples. Cut out 4 circles of pastry, large enough to wrap round each apple completely in a single, even layer; don't get the pastry too thick. Put an apple onto each of the pastry circles and fill the centre of each one with raisins. Brush the edges of the circles with water and bring the pastry up around each apple, sealing it as best you can.

Turn and mould each apple gently in your hands until you can't see the join. As you do this you may find you need to trim away any overlapping pieces of pastry. Use these for leaves, if you are making them. Brush them with water and roll them carefully in caster sugar; stick the loaves on at this stage, and then very carefully transfer the apples to the tray.

Bake for 20–25 minutes or until the pastry is golden and the apples are cooked through.

Serve warm, rather than hot, with custard or cream.

SERVES 4

Pastry, as for **Old-Fashioned Apple Plate Pie**, above
4 dessert apples
110g (4oz) raisins
Unrefined caster sugar for rolling

You will need a greased baking tray

CHRISTMAS APPLE DUMPLINGS

You can make a couple of very Christmassy versions of apple dumplings. Instead of filling the centre of the apples with raisins, fill with either mincemeat or marzipan (preferably home-made versions!) and prepare and cook as above. The mincemeat ones are particularly good with custard and the marzipan ones are particularly good with cream.

TURNOVERS

A turnover is a really simple kind of pastry to do. You can cut out neat circles, or you can just roll your pastry into a ball and roll it out flat into a rough circle. For this reason a turnover is an ideal way to use up leftover pastry. You can make little mini pasties out of the leftovers, or make a little apple turnover out of any leftovers from an apple pie.

Alternatively, if you would like a triangular turnover, you can cut your pastry out in squares, to flip over into triangles. If you are careful, you'll have hardly any wastage this way either.

Usually, turnovers are 'crimped' (or sealed by pressing down lightly with a fork) at the side, but if you are using jam as a filling, try to make your crimp at the top, as jam turns to boiling liquid very quickly in a hot oven and will run out of the turnover if you're not careful. For this reason, never attempt to eat a jam turnover straight out of the oven!

Suggested fillings for turnovers
• A few thin slices of apple moistened with the tiniest amount of apple juice or water;
• A spoonful or two of mincemeat;
• Some thin slices of apple *and* mincemeat together;
• A dollop of jam such as raspberry, strawberry or apricot, or marmalade.

MINCE PIES

If you are making your own mince pies, it's important that the pastry is really special and delicious; a bit like shortbread, in fact. This is an all-butter pastry, with a bit more butter and a bit less water than usual. It's easier to make sweet pastry extra nice as the sugar adds to the crumbly texture.

Preheat oven to 180°C (fan oven) or equivalent.

Sieve the flour and salt carefully into the bowl of your food processor and add the butter. Whiz into fine crumbs and add the sugar. Whiz again briefly. Add the water and whiz until the mixture is starting to come together. Turn it out onto a floured board and knead it lightly until it forms a ball.

Roll it out gently with a floured rolling pin to a thickness of just less than ½cm (¼in).

Cut out 12 circles with the larger cutter (for the pies) and 12 circles with the smaller cutter (for the lids). As you put the larger circles into the tart tins, firm them down gently so that the finished pies will be a good shape rather than just a little saucer of pastry!

Put about a teaspoon of mincemeat into each: don't overfill as the mincemeat will boil out. Brush the edge of each lid with water and press them gently onto the pies. Brush each pie with water and sprinkle a little caster sugar over the top. Make a little hole in each lid with the point of a knife.

Bake for about 12 minutes or until pale golden. Remove from the tin and cool on a wire rack.

MAKES 12

175g (6oz) plain flour
Pinch salt
110g (4oz) cold butter
25g (1oz) unrefined caster sugar
1 tablespoon cold water
12 teaspoons of mincemeat (see below)

A little more caster sugar for finishing

You will need 2 fluted cutters, 7½cm (3in) and 6cm (2½in), and a greased 12-cup tart tin

HOME-MADE MINCEMEAT

Home-made mincemeat is far better than anything you can buy ready made. It needs a good two weeks for the flavours to develop properly so if you are making it for Christmas, aim to make it between mid and late November. It's very easy: just a bit of weighing, chopping and stirring.

MAKES approximately 1.5 kilos (a little over 3lb)

225g (8oz) raisins
225g (8oz) sultanas
225g (8oz) currants
225g (8oz) soft dark brown sugar
225g (8oz) firm dessert apples such as Cox's, peeled and cored (prepared weight)
175g (6oz) shredded suet
110g (4oz) candied peel, cut into fine pieces
Finely grated zest and juice of 1 orange
Finely grated zest and juice of 1 lemon
2–3 teaspoons mixed spice
150ml (¼ pint) brandy

Put everything into a large bowl; a casserole dish with a lid is ideal. When you add the apples, grate them onto a clean board and make sure you include all their juice. Strain the orange and lemon juice through a sieve and zest the peel into short pieces rather then long strands. Mix everything together thoroughly and leave overnight in a cool place for the flavours to amalgamate. The next day give everything a stir and spoon into sterilised jars. Try to avoid leaving any air pockets: keep turning the jars round to check and push the mincemeat down with a knife if you see any.

To sterilise the jars
Wash the jars in hot soapy water and rinse thoroughly. Shake off any excess water and stand on a baking tray. Put into the oven for 10 minutes or so at 160ºC or equivalent. Alternatively, you can put them through the hottest cycle of your dishwasher if you have one.

MINCEMEAT TART

This is a great tart served warm for a winter pudding with custard, or cold as a teatime treat. If you are serving it cold you might like to drizzle it with glacé icing and decorate it with a few walnut or pecan halves. The all-butter shortcrust pastry is slightly less rich than the mince pie pastry. Alternatively use plain shortcrust: see **Savoury Flans** *for more detail.*

Preheat oven to 190ºC (fan oven) or equivalent.

Sieve the flour and salt carefully into the bowl of your food processor and add the butter. Whiz into fine crumbs and add the sugar. Whiz again briefly. Add the water and whiz until the mixture is starting to come together. Turn it out onto a floured board and knead it lightly until it forms a ball.

Roll it out gently with a floured rolling pin to a thickness of just less than 1cm.

Line the flan tin and bake blind for approximately 15 minutes: see **Savoury Flans** for more details.

Once the pastry case is ready, reduce the oven temperature to 180ºC (fan oven) or equivalent, fill the pastry case with the mincemeat and return to the oven for 10 minutes, until the mincemeat is cooked through.

There should be enough pastry left over to make a handful of jam tarts or a couple of mince pies as well.

✔ **Useful Note** Try this if you find yourself with nearly, but not quite, enough mincemeat to make the tart or a few more mince pies. Stir a little orange juice and some raisins and sultanas into whatever mincemeat you have left: if you need to stretch it further add half a grated or finely chopped apple as well.

For the pastry
175g (6oz) plain flour
Pinch salt
75g (3oz) cold butter
25g (1oz) unrefined caster
   sugar
3 tablespoons cold water

For the filling
5–6 tablespoons
   mincemeat

You will need a 20cm (8in)
   greased flan tin

Jam Tarts

*I remember making these at school once when I was about six. I say making them; actually, I think we just watched as our teacher did all the work. We did get to eat one each though when they had cooled down enough and they were just fabulous. I've loved jam tarts ever since. The trouble is that when you are six, a jam tart seems quite big but when you are grown up they seem to have got a lot smaller! If you prefer, you can make them with plain unsweetened shortcrust: see **Savoury Flans** or **Treacle Tart**.*

MAKES about 16	Preheat oven to 180ºC (fan ovens) or equivalent.
For the pastry Make the same pastry as for the **Mincemeat Tart** above. You may want to make a double batch; if so make each batch separately as the average food processor works best with no more than a 175g (6oz) mix at a time.	Turn the pastry out onto a floured board and knead it lightly until it forms a ball. Roll it out gently with a floured rolling pin to a thickness of just less than ½cm (⅛in.). Cut out circles and put into the prepared tins; firm them down gently so that the finished tarts will be a good shape rather than just little saucers of pastry.
Plus: jam to fill the tarts; raspberry, strawberry, apricot and blackcurrant all work well	Fill each tart with no more than a slightly rounded teaspoon of jam: they need to be generously filled but not so much that as the jam heats up it boils out of the tarts. Bake for 10–12 minutes until the pastry is lightly golden. Keep the tart tins level as you take them out of the oven; if you tilt them the practically molten jam can spill out of the tarts at this stage. Remove from the tin with a small palette knife and cool on a wire rack.
You will need a 7½cm (3in) fluted cutter and a greased 12-cup tart tin	**Caution: on no account eat the tarts while the jam is still hot!**

Treacle Tart

This was something else that featured in my mum's cookery book: we did actually make this and it was a big success. I can remember being surprised that the treacle part contained breadcrumbs: I'd often wondered how the treacle got so bumpy! Serve warm or cold with custard or clotted cream. The pastry is a plain unsweetened shortcrust, as the filling (which is slightly adapted from the original) is rather sweet.

To make the pastry

Preheat the oven to 190ºC (fan oven) or equivalent.

Sieve the flour carefully into the bowl of your food processor and add the butter, vegetable shortening and salt. Whiz into fine crumbs. Add the water and whiz again. Once it is starting to form big crumbs and clump together, turn it out onto a lightly floured board and knead it gently into a ball.

Try to keep it round and roll it gently with a lightly floured rolling pin into a large disc of roughly ½cm (¼in.) thick. Roll it round your rolling pin and manoeuvre it gently off the rolling pin and on top of the prepared flan tin. Hold the sides upright as best you can while you settle it into the bottom of the tin, firming gently with your fingers. Trim away the excess. Prick the bottom lightly all over with a fork.

Put a circle of greaseproof paper on the bottom of the pastry case and fill it to the top with baking beans (see page 186 'Baking blind'). Bake for 20 minutes. Leave to settle for a few moments and remove the beans from the pastry case (tip them out very gently into something such as a fairly wide metal colander until they cool down, taking care not to damage the edge of the pastry).

To make the filling

Reduce oven temperature to 180ºC (fan oven) or equivalent.

Warm the golden syrup and brown sugar gently in a fairly roomy saucepan over a moderate heat for a couple of minutes until it is of pouring consistency. This will take a little longer in cool weather as the syrup will be firmer to start with.

Remove from the heat and stir in the lemon juice, vanilla and salt. Once the lemon juice is all incorporated, stir in the breadcrumbs, a few at a time, so they are all coated with syrup. Spoon the mixture into the prepared pastry case and smooth into position. Bake for around 30 minutes, until the top is very slightly browning.

✓ Useful Note: Making the breadcrumbs

Remove the crusts from the bread and tear into pieces. Whiz briefly in the food processor until fine.

For the pastry
175g (6oz) plain flour
40g (1½oz) butter, cold and cut into small pieces
40g (1½oz) block vegetable shortening, cold and cut into small pieces
Pinch of salt
3 tablespoons cold water

For the filling
4 tablespoons golden syrup
40g (1½oz) soft dark brown sugar
Juice of 1 lemon, sieved
1 teaspoon vanilla extract
Pinch of salt
About 110g (4oz) white or light wholemeal breadcrumbs (no crusts)

You will need a greased 20cm (8in) loose-bottomed flan tin

LITTLE TREACLE TARTS

These are made in exactly the same way as above. There is no need to bake blind: they are so small the filling and pastry can cook together. It's useful if you have a second tart tin so you can bake them all in one go, otherwise bake a second part batch.

MAKES 16

You will need a greased
  12-cup tart tin

Cut out circles of pastry using a 7½cm (3in) fluted cutter and put into the prepared tins. Firm them down gently so that the finished tarts will be a good shape rather than just little saucers of pastry. Put a teaspoonful of the treacle mixture into each tart.

Bake as for the **Treacle Tart** for about 15 minutes, remove from the tin with a small palette knife and cool on a wire rack.

BISCUITS

Biscuits are very easy and satisfying to make. The main thing that can go wrong with biscuits is that it is very easy to overcook them so they are burnt and bitter. It can literally take just *one single minute* for biscuits to be overcooked and ruined. You need to use a timer and to stay within earshot.

When biscuits first come out of the oven they are still soft and it's easy to think they aren't cooked. They will soon harden as they cool down. Some biscuits are meant to be more of a slightly chewy cookie consistency rather than crisp and brittle. It pays to know your oven so make notes of cooking times and temperatures that work for a particular recipe in your oven and refer back to them.

Oven temperatures
Please be aware that individual oven performance can vary tremendously. With the exception of shortbread and oatcakes, an average temperature of 180ºC or equivalent has been suggested for recipes in this section. Some ovens may need to be set higher or lower.

CHOCOLATE BISCUITS

These biscuits are very simple to make: they aren't too sweet and have a beautiful deep chocolatey taste. They lend themselves to all kinds of shaped cutters and are fun for children to make. Unfortunately, the dough tastes very good raw, so be prepared to sustain some losses!

You can mix the dough perfectly well by hand but it's very quick and easy in the food processor.

MAKES up to 30 biscuits, depending on cutter size

110g (4oz) softened butter
50g (2oz) unrefined caster sugar
160g (5½oz) plain flour
2 heaped tablespoons cocoa powder
(Combined weight of flour and cocoa together should be 200g (7oz))
2 tablespoons semi-skimmed milk

You will need a large greased baking tray

Preheat oven to 180ºC (fan oven) or equivalent.

Whiz the butter and sugar together and sieve in the flour and cocoa. Whiz again. Add the milk and whiz until the mixture comes together and forms a large ball. Stop the machine immediately at this point: if you over-process the dough it will become overstretched and unmanageable.

Roll out onto a lightly floured board using a lightly floured rolling pin to about ½cm (¼in.) thick. Cut out using any shaped cutter that you like and arrange on the greased baking tray. Re-roll the trimmings until you have used up all the dough.

Bake for approximately 8 minutes (non-fan ovens may need a little longer). Almost immediately lift from the tray with a small palette knife and cool on a wire rack.

✓ **Useful Note** Sometimes, particularly if the weather is quite warm, the mixture may feel a little sticky and be difficult to roll. In this case you can chill it in the fridge for up to half an hour. Alternatively, you may find that just sieving a little more flour over the mixture and re-rolling it will do the trick.

Once you get your biscuits on the tray, you may find that they look a bit dusty and floury on top. Just brush them over with milk: they will then come out of the oven with a nice sheen to them.

To ice the biscuits
Occasionally, you might want to ice these biscuits. A simple white glacé icing works best. You can just drizzle lines across the biscuits or get a bit more creative if you are handy with an icing nozzle. One nice idea, if you happen to have a cow-shaped cutter, is to splodge little patches over them so they look like a herd of Friesians!

For the glacé icing

The lemon juice just takes the edge off the sweetness.

110g (4oz) icing sugar
1–2 tablespoons lemon
juice

Sieve the icing sugar into a bowl and stir in a tablespoon or two of lemon juice, beat it with a wooden spoon until smooth and glossy: make a fairly stiff yet workable mixture. Drizzle or 'splodge' the icing over the biscuits: either use an icing bag or let it drizzle off a teaspoon.

To make Chocolate Fork Biscuits

Fork biscuits are easy to make and look most professional. Roll the dough into small balls and press down with the back of a fork. Most firm biscuit dough will work as fork biscuits.

To make Chocolate Dinosaur Bones and Chocolate Fossils

These look really funny and are great for children, both to eat and to make (and to use up the last of the dough). It's hard to describe the method but take a small amount of dough and squeeze it quite hard in the palm of your hand so that it just starts to squeeze between your fingers. With a bit of imagination, the finished result looks a bit like a dinosaur bone or fossil! Bake with the rest of the biscuits.

Using fancy cutters

There are lots of fancy-shaped cutters in the shops and it is fun to build up a collection. Just a word of warning, though: the more intricate the shape, the more difficult and time-consuming the biscuits will be to cut out. Be prepared for anxious moments with narrow little legs and ears and so forth coming adrift. Sometimes it is possible to open out the narrow bits on cutters a little more with the handle of a teaspoon. Also, roll your dough out slightly thicker than normal.

Useful Note You can store the dough in the fridge for a few days or freeze it. Defrost frozen dough overnight in the fridge and take dough out of the fridge 20 minutes or so before you need to use it.

GENTLY SPICED BISCUITS

These have a lovely flavour and make great gingerbread men. You can cut them out in any shape you like to appeal to adults or children: circles, fingers, animals, hearts or stars, whatever you fancy. They make good Hallowe'en and Christmas cookies too.

MAKES approximately 30 biscuits, depending on cutter size	Preheat oven to 180ºC (fan oven) or equivalent.
	Whiz the butter and sugar together in the food processor. Add the flours, salt and spices and beaten egg and whiz until the mixture forms large clumps and begins to gather together. Stop the processor, remove the blade and finish gently kneading the dough together on a lightly floured board.
150g (5oz) softened butter	
150g (5oz) unrefined caster sugar	
150g (5oz) plain flour	
50g (2oz) wholemeal plain flour	Roll out the dough with a lightly floured rolling pin to roughly ½cm (¼in.) thick: you may want to work in two batches. Cut out the biscuits with your chosen cutter and bake for about 7 minutes or until pale golden and very, very slightly brown at the edges. Remove from the tray with a small palette knife and cool on a wire rack. Once cold, store in an airtight container.
Pinch of salt	
1½ teaspoons each of ground mixed spice, ginger and cinnamon	
1 egg, lightly beaten	
You will need a large greased baking tray	You can store the uncooked dough in the fridge for a few days or freeze it. Defrost frozen dough overnight in the fridge and take it out of the fridge 20 minutes or so before you need to use it.

EXTRA BROWN GENTLY SPICED BISCUITS

These are the same as the above recipe but instead of unrefined caster sugar use the same amount of **soft dark brown sugar**. This gives the biscuits a greater depth of flavour and a slightly darker brown colour. For an even darker biscuit and deeper, treacly flavour, use **muscovado sugar**.

ORANGE BISCUITS

These are lovely, light biscuits, perfect with a cup of tea or coffee. You can mix them by hand but it's much easier in a food processor. Be sure to use fresh oranges: nothing shrunken and wizened!

Preheat oven to 180°C (fan ovens) or equivalent.

Put the butter and sugar in the bowl of your food processor and whiz until light and fluffy. Add the egg and orange zest and sieve about half the flour and baking powder carefully over the top. Whiz until everything is starting to come together and then add the rest of the flour; again, sieving it carefully. Whiz until the mixture starts to clump together, then stop the machine. You may have to do this in stages as the mixture is quite dense, removing the lid and scraping the mixture down from the sides three or four times, particularly at the beginning.

Scoop the mixture out of the machine and knead it lightly together on a floured board. Divide it into two pieces and make the biscuits in two batches. Roll the first piece out to a thickness of about ½cm. Cut out rounds with a plain 6cm (2½in) cutter. Transfer to the prepared baking sheet: use a palette knife to help you as the mixture is quite delicate.

Bake for 5–7 minutes until the biscuits are pale golden, but not at all brown.

Repeat for the second batch. If you prefer you can store the dough in the fridge for a few days or freeze it. Defrost frozen dough overnight in the fridge and take dough out of the fridge 20 minutes or so before you need to use it.

Leave to cool for a couple of minutes, no longer, on the tray, and then transfer to a cooling rack, using a palette knife. The biscuits are very soft when they come out of the oven, but will harden as they cool. Once they are completely cold, store in an airtight tin.

✓ **Useful Note** Leave space between the biscuits as they are the type that spread out quite a bit during baking. For this reason it would be difficult to cut them out in any shape other than approximately round!

MAKES approximately 34 biscuits

150g (5oz) butter, softened
110g (4oz) unrefined caster sugar
1 egg, beaten
Finely grated zest of 2 oranges
200g (7oz) plain flour
2 teaspoons baking powder

You will need a large greased baking tray

LEMON BISCUITS

These are made in exactly the same way as the **Orange Biscuits** above, but use the zest of 2 lemons instead of oranges. They are lovely with a cup of tea or served with a light pudding for a posh dinner. As with the **Orange Biscuits**, be sure to choose plump fresh lemons for the best zest.

SHORTBREAD

You can make this entirely by hand if you prefer but it's easier to get it started in the food processor and finish it by hand. Don't try to do the whole operation in the food processor, though, as it will become over-processed and 'overstretched'! It should still be very pale and even-coloured once it is cooked.

MAKES 8 pieces	Preheat oven to 150ºC (fan oven) or equivalent.

175g (6oz) plain flour
110g (4oz) butter, cut into
   small pieces
50g (2oz) unrefined caster
   sugar
	Carefully sieve the flour into the bowl of your processor with the butter. Whiz briefly until it resembles fairly coarse crumbs. Add the sugar and whiz again. Take the lid off and give the mixture a stir.

You will need a greased baking tray	Continue whizzing, stopping a couple of times to stir the mixture round, until it is just starting to clump together. Remove the blade from the machine and put the mixture onto a clean board; you won't need to flour it.
	Gather the mixture into a ball and gently knead it with your hands. It will take a couple of minutes, or even a little longer, but the warmth from your hands and the kneading action will eventually bind it together. When you first start, this will seem pretty unlikely, as it just seems like a mass of crumbs, which will then become an unwieldy sausage shape, but before long it will be starting to come together into a satisfying ball. Continue until you have what looks and feels like a ball of marzipan.
	Once you have got to this stage, flatten it slightly with your hands so that it is a fairly thick disc and transfer it to the greased baking tray. Once it is on the tray, roll it gently with a lightly floured rolling pin until you have a disc that is a little larger than 18cm (7in) in diameter and roughly 1cm thick.

Even the edges with your hands and indent them slightly with the balls of your thumbs and then pinch the edges slightly with your thumb and forefinger until you have something resembling the traditional round of Petticoat Tails shortbread. This will have the effect of making your disc slightly smaller and thicker again.

Prick all over the top with a fork and mark into 8 segments with a knife, but don't cut all the way through. If you are worried about scratching your baking tray, use one of those fairly substantial plastic picnic knives with a serrated edge.

Bake for about 30 minutes until very pale golden but not at all brown. Sprinkle with caster sugar while warm. Cool on a wire tray and cut into segments. Once cool store in an airtight tin.

This will give you a crisp, biscuity shortbread with a crisp snap. If you prefer a more crumbly, less crisp texture, bake for the same amount of time at 140ºC (fan oven) or equivalent.

LEMON SHORTBREAD

The lemony tang contrasts well with the rich buttery taste of the shortbread. Make it in the same way as the previous recipe but add the **finely grated zest of 1 lemon** when you add the sugar to the mix. Bake as above. Sprinkle with caster sugar, cool on a wire rack and store in an airtight tin. The lemon flavour will be more pronounced the next day.

CRANBERRY AND LEMON SHORTBREAD

Cranberries and lemons just go together so beautifully! Make this in the same way as the **Lemon Shortbread** above, but knead **25–50g (1–2oz) dried cranberries** into the mix once you have taken it out of the machine and it still hasn't quite come together.

SHREWSBURY TYPE BISCUITS

This is a really adaptable Shrewsbury type biscuit recipe. You can cut the biscuits out with a fluted round cutter or, if you are making them with or for children, you can use novelty cutters instead. The biscuits are lovely plain, or you can flavour them more specifically with the finely grated zest of a lemon, ½ teaspoon of mixed spice, or ½ teaspoon of vanilla extract or vanilla bean paste. A little white caster sugar sifted over these biscuits is a nice touch.

MAKES approximately 24 biscuits, depending on cutter size

110g (4oz) softened butter
75g (3oz) unrefined caster sugar
200g (7oz) plain flour
2 eggs: 1 whole egg and 1 egg yolk, beaten

You will need a large greased baking tray

Preheat oven to 180°C (fan oven) or equivalent.

Put the softened butter and sugar in a large bowl and cream together with a wooden spoon until completely mixed together and fluffy. Sieve the flour (and spice, if using) over the mixture and add the egg and egg yolk.

Stir together with the wooden spoon until it is fairly well mixed and most of the flour has been absorbed. You will need to finish the mixing by hand now: the warmth from your hands will help bind everything together.

Put the mixture onto a floured board and continue to knead it until you have what looks (and feels) like a large ball of marzipan. Roll out with a floured rolling pin to a thickness of a bit more than a pound coin. Cut out with your chosen cutters and put onto the prepared baking tray.

Bake for 7–8 minutes or until very pale golden. Remove fairly swiftly from the baking tray with a small palette knife, and cool on a wire rack. Sprinkle with caster sugar, if liked. Once cooled, the biscuits will keep in an airtight tin for several days.

You can store the uncooked dough in the fridge for a few days or freeze it. Defrost frozen dough overnight in the fridge and take dough out of the fridge 20 minutes or so before you need to use it.

FRUIT SHREWSBURY BISCUITS

If you would like a fruit biscuit, stir in 50g (2oz) of currants. When you roll the dough and cut the biscuits out, try not to have any currants 'proud' of the mixture as they will bake too hard to eat.

EASTER BISCUITS

The Shrewsbury Biscuit recipe also makes great Easter Biscuits. These are usually gently spiced so add ½ teaspoon of mixed spice. You can use a round cutter or some novelty Easter shapes. Again, a dusting of white caster sugar adds the finishing touch.

OATY BISCUITS

These are delicious crunchy biscuits, not too rich, with a lovely flavour. They are a welcome treat with a cup of tea or coffee or slipped into a child's lunch box.

Preheat oven to 180ºC (fan oven) or equivalent.	MAKES about 30
Melt the butter, sugar and golden syrup together over a gentle heat. Stir in the vanilla and then the oats, finally stir in the wholemeal flour and sieve in the self-raising flour. Mix everything together thoroughly.	110g (4oz) butter 110g (4oz) soft light brown sugar 2 generous tablespoons golden syrup ½–1 teaspoon vanilla extract 110g (4oz) porridge oats 50g (2oz) wholemeal flour 110g (4oz) self-raising flour
Lift the mixture onto a lightly floured board and knead gently. Roll to a thickness of slightly less than ½cm with a lightly floured rolling pin and cut into rounds.	
You may need a palette knife to help you lift the biscuits onto the baking tray as the dough is quite soft. They will spread very slightly during baking so leave a little space between them.	
Bake for 6–8 minutes or until a nice even golden colour: don't let the edges go brown or they will be too hard. Remove from the baking tray with a palette knife and cool on a wire rack. Once cold, store in an airtight tin.	You will need a large greased baking tray

FRUITY OATY BISCUITS

Make these in exactly the same way as the **Oaty Biscuits** above but add **50g (2oz) raisins** with the butter, sugar and syrup as they melt: this will give the raisins a chance to plump up a bit. Continue as above. As with any biscuit containing dried fruit, when you roll out the dough try not to have any raisins 'proud' of the mixture or they will bake too hard to eat.

VERY SIMPLE OATCAKES

These oatcakes are very simple indeed! They contain only oatmeal and water, with perhaps a little salt if you are feeling fancy.

MAKES 15

225g (8oz) medium
    oatmeal, plus quite a bit
    more for rolling
75ml (3fl oz) warm water
Pinch of salt, if liked

You will need a large
    greased baking tray

Preheat oven to 200ºC (fan oven) or equivalent.

Put the oatmeal into a roomy bowl and mix in the warm water with a wooden spoon. If you are using salt, dissolve it in the water first. You will notice an encouraging and appetising nutty smell at this stage.

Spread some more oatmeal onto your board or work surface and rub some onto your hands (it will all fall off but you will be left with a faint powdery coating). Shape the mixture in the bowl into a ball and pour a little more oatmeal over it.

Lift it onto the board and, making sure it is completely coated in oatmeal, roll it to about the thickness of a pound coin. Cut into rounds using a plain round, not fluted, 7½cm (3in) cutter. Transfer to the greased baking tray and bake for 15 minutes, turning the biscuits over halfway, after 7 or 8 minutes. Cool on a wire rack.

These are really delicious with butter and honey or any kind of cheese. They will keep for several days in an airtight container.

✓ **Useful Notes** The water must be warm for this recipe as it seems to meld the oatmeal together. Cold water doesn't bring the mixture together properly and it will be too crumbly to work with.

If you are left with a lot of oaty crumbs at the end, put them back in the bowl and moisten with a drop more warm water, then you can re-roll it. Take your time with these. It may seem a bit of a fiddle but the fascination is in making something really good from two such simple ingredients.

CHEESY BISCUITS

This is a really versatile recipe: the biscuits can be cut out in serious plain shapes for adults or seriously silly shapes for children. If you are having a children's party you can theme the shape to the party (such as cheesy fish for a pirate party) or you can make the biscuits look elegant as little nibbles for a grown-up affair (see below). Use smallish cutters as the biscuits are rather rich.

Preheat oven to 180°C (fan oven) or equivalent.

Sieve the flour and mustard powder carefully into the bowl of your food processor, sprinkle in the salt and add the butter. Give the mixture a quick whiz to start everything off and add the cheese (the lesser amount of cheese will make a slightly less rich biscuit, the greater amount will be a little cheesier and richer).

Keep whizzing, stopping from time to time to remove the lid and give the mixture a quick stir, until the mixture starts to clump together. Stop the machine, remove the blade and transfer the mixture to a clean board.

Gently bring the mixture together with your hands and knead it lightly until it looks and feels like a ball of cheesy marzipan. Flour the board lightly and, using a floured rolling pin, roll out to a thickness of just less than ½cm (¼in.). Cut out your shapes and arrange on the prepared tray. Re-roll and cut out the rest. If you have any dough left over, roll it into little balls and flatten with your hand or a fork and bake with the others.

Bake for 7–8 minutes, or until the biscuits are golden in colour. Remove from the oven and leave to settle for a few moments. Remove from the tray carefully with a palette knife and finish cooling on a wire rack. Store in an airtight tin.

MAKES about 15
depending on cutter size

50g (2oz) plain flour
Pinch of dry mustard
powder
Pinch of salt
25g (1oz) butter, softened
75–110g (3–4oz) grated
well-flavoured Cheddar
cheese

You will need a large
greased baking tray and
some biscuit cutters

CHEESY CHILLI BISCUITS

The mustard powder in the above recipe is really just to bring out the flavour of the cheese but if you would like something a bit more challenging, add a full ¼ teaspoon of mustard powder and ¼ teaspoon of chilli powder to the flour at the beginning. Cheese and chilli are always a great combination. Alternatively, for posh nibbles, instead of cutting them out, flatten balls of dough with a fork, as above, and sprinkle with a little cayenne or paprika while they are still warm. Sesame seeds are great (although admittedly a bit of a fiddle) sprinkled over the biscuits before they go into the oven: brush the biscuits with water first.

MAKING YOUR OWN BREAD AT HOME WITH A BREAD MACHINE

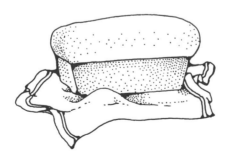

Making your own bread at home is really easy if you have a bread machine. You hear stories all the time about people who have a machine that is stuffed into the back of a cupboard and never used. More than likely, this is because they have never given themselves a chance to get used to it. Making your own bread means that you can have delicious, additive-free bread (organic if you like) whenever you want. You don't have to go and fetch it from the shops and it will cost half as much or less than ready-made.

You might not know this, but most bread machines have a quick or rapid programme that takes a fraction under two hours. This makes a milder, less yeasty tasting loaf that you might like better, at first anyway. If you are hopeless at slicing bread, you can buy a slicing machine for quite a lot less money than a pair of children's shoes. Also, if you invest in a large plastic sandwich box style bread bin, your bread will keep fresh for a few days. Apart from ready-baked loaves, your bread machine will also mix the dough for you to make your own buns, rolls and pizza bases.

So, what do you have to do? Invest in a decent machine and unless none of the family likes dried fruit, buy the type with the raisin option, as it will be really useful. Make a permanent place for it out on the worktop, so it is handy and available. Finally, and this is the most crucial bit, give yourself a few days to get to know how it works, practise making several loaves, and get into a routine with it. It only takes two minutes, literally, to put the ingredients into the machine. Get into the habit of putting a loaf on when you know you will be around two hours later to take it out: that's all it takes!

Finally, a lot of people say, 'Oh, we couldn't possibly have freshly baked bread in the house; we would just eat it all the time. Well, firstly, you won't (at least, not after the first few times, anyway) and also it seems a bit silly, doesn't it, to be saying, in effect, you mustn't have bread that is too nice!

A bread machine really does make things easier, but once you get started you might enjoy it so much that you'll be making your own bread entirely by hand before long!

For this section, several of the recipes are very similar so it won't take long to build up a small repertoire of loaves and rolls, buns and pizza dough. Some of the recipes are made entirely in the machine and some just use the machine to make the dough. Make sure when you buy white flour it is **strong bread flour** and that you buy **quick yeast made for use in bread machines.**

It is worth remembering that whilst a cake will do all its rising *inside* the oven, bread does the majority of its rising *before* it goes into the oven.

Oven temperatures

Oven performance can vary tremendously. Some ovens will happily bake bread at 180ºC but it is more usual to bake bread at 200–220ºC or equivalent. For this reason, with the exception of Panettone and Pizzas, baking temperatures in this section are given as 180–220ºC or equivalent. Practice will tell which is correct for your oven.

Easy White Loaf

This recipe uses the 'quick loaf' or 'rapid bake' programme (see above). The water should be warm to activate the yeast properly. You could warm it in the microwave for 30–40 seconds on High.

Put the yeast, salt and sugar into the bread pan of your machine and put the flour on top. Pour in the warm water and the oil. Set the machine to the **quick loaf** programme and in less than two hours you will have a lovely fresh loaf.

Once the loaf is ready, take it out of the machine and slide it out, on its side, onto a wooden board. Pick it up and stand it upright on a cooling rack. Once it is completely cold, store it in an airtight plastic box or a sealed plastic bag. If you are going to slice it by machine wait a few hours as it is difficult to slice it properly when it is very fresh.

Never ease a loaf out with a knife or anything metal or you will damage the inside of your bread pan. Sometimes, the mixing blade can get stuck in the loaf. Once the loaf is cool it's easy to get it out with your fingers; again, don't use anything metal as you will scratch the blade. Incidentally, if you leave the loaf in the machine for too long once it is ready, it will go damp and wrinkly. It will still be edible but not *quite* as nice.

Weather warning During hot, sultry summer days bread – home-made bread in particular – will not keep as long as during cooler weather and can be prone to mould.

1 teaspoon quick yeast
1 teaspoon salt
1 tablespoon unrefined granulated sugar
385g (14oz) strong white bread flour
300ml (11fl oz) warm water
2 tablespoons mild, flavourless oil, such as mild olive, sunflower or rapeseed

Easy Wholemeal Loaf

This is just the same as the previous recipe, but include 75–110g (3–4oz) of wholemeal flour as part of your flour measurement.

EASY SEED AND GRAIN LOAF

Again this is very similar but use 75–110g (3–4oz) of malted multi-grain flour instead of wholemeal. In addition to this you can add a handful of seeds to the mixture as well. Sunflower seeds, pumpkin seeds, linseed and hemp seeds are all good. If you add them at the start they will be ground into the dough so you won't be able to see separate discernible seeds but it will still taste good. If you would like the seeds to stay in one piece, you can wait until near the end of the kneading process and add them then. With some machines this is 12 minutes into the programme so you could set a kitchen timer for 12 minutes as soon as the bread machine is switched on. Once the time is up, open the lid of the bread machine and tip in the seeds. Experiment with your own machine and keep notes. Alternatively, you can select the Raisin Bake programme and put your seeds into the raisin compartment. This programme will take longer, usually about four hours.

EASY POTATO LOAF

This loaf contains a relatively small amount of potato, but enough to make a difference. The finished loaf is fluffy and moist: it's beautiful eaten fresh with butter and it makes great toast the following day.

---

1 teaspoon quick yeast
1 teaspoon salt
1 tablespoon sugar
385g (14oz) strong white
  bread flour
110g (4oz) leftover
  cooked potatoes,
  mashed or boiled
160ml (5–6fl oz) cooking
  water from the
  potatoes, slightly warm
2–3 tablespoons mild oil

Put the yeast, salt and sugar into the bread pan of your machine and put the flour on top. Add the potatoes; if they are not already mashed, mash them with a fork. Pour in the potato water and the oil. Set the machine to the **quick loaf** programme.

✔ **Useful Note** Incidentally, potato water instead of plain water will give any loaf an extra lightness. Alternatively, if you make your own soft cheese or thick yoghurt (the sort where you drain off the whey through muslin) keep the whey and use that to make your bread. It works even more magically than potato water.

Easy Fruit Bread

You will need to experiment a bit with your bread machine to find out exactly when is the right time within the kneading cycle to add the fruit during the **quick loaf** programme. Use the **Easy White Loaf** recipe and set your kitchen timer to the correct time for your machine (see above) as soon as you switch the bread machine on.

Measure out about 225g (8oz) of mixed dried fruit – currants, raisins and sultanas – and have them ready. The moment the time is up, lift the lid of the machine and tip the fruit in. The advantage of this method rather than the Raisin Bake option is that apart from taking a shorter time, you can get more fruit in, as the raisin compartment can only accommodate a relatively small amount.

Rolls, Baps and Buns

MAKES 12

1 tablespoon sugar
1¾ teaspoons quick yeast
1 teaspoon salt
500g (1lb 2oz) strong
    white bread flour
330ml (10?fl oz))
    lukewarm water or milk
2–3 tablespoons mild oil

You will need a large
    greased baking tray

Put the sugar, yeast and salt in separate corners of the bread pan, add the flour and the warm water on top, pour in the oil. Set your machine to the **dough** setting: normally this will be about 45 minutes.

Once the dough is ready, turn it out onto a floured board and cut the dough into 12 fairly even pieces; there is no need to knead it further. Shape the dough into roll shapes: round or sausage shapes for rolls and flatter rounds for baps. Space them out evenly on the baking tray and leave them in a warm place for an hour or so until doubled in size.

Bake in a preheated oven at 180–220ºC (fan oven) or equivalent, for 8–10 minutes until golden brown. Leave on the baking tray for a few moments and then remove and cool on a wire rack. A clean tea towel over the top will keep them fresh and moist as they cool.

Once you have got the hang of these you might like to try experimenting with other types of flour. You could replace 75–110g (3–4oz) of white flour with spelt flour or buckwheat or rye. Malted grain and barleycorn mixes are also good. Alternatively, try kamut flour: like spelt, this is another ancient, wheat-type grain; it is particularly high in selenium, which many modern diets can lack, and has a lovely sweet taste.

Sesame Seed Buns and Other Topped Rolls

You can also top these rolls with different seeds or oat flakes. Brush the tops of the buns lightly with water (or mist lightly with water from a clean spray bottle) before they go into the oven and sprinkle the seeds or oats on top. You can make classic burger buns by making bap shapes, brushing with water and sprinkling with sesame seeds.

You might like to make the rolls a little smaller: divide the dough into 24 and push them together on the tray in a joined batch. You can also push them together and bake them in a shallow roasting tin.

Rolls in a Bun Tin and 'Splits'

These rolls have a really appealing shape and are very easy to make. Although these are a regular roll, the recipe is actually very similar to that for Devonshire or Cornish Splits: soft white rolls split and eaten with clotted cream and jam. They make a lovely alternative to scones. If you are going to eat them like this, sieve a little white flour over the top of each one, using a teaspoon and a small sieve or tea strainer, and eat them while they are very fresh.

The mixture is the same as for the rolls recipe above.	Once the dough is ready, turn it out onto a floured board and cut the dough into 12 fairly even pieces. Roll each piece lightly in the flour on the board and put into a greased 12-cup bun or muffin tin.
You will need a greased 12-cup bun or muffin tin	Leave in a warm place for a couple of hours, covered lightly in greaseproof paper, until the rolls have doubled in size. This step is crucial: **they must be risen before you put them in the oven**, otherwise they will be like little rocks! Preheat oven to 180–220°C (fan oven) or equivalent. Bake for about 8 minutes or until the rolls are lightly golden. Incidentally, once the rolls have doubled in size, get them in the oven pretty quickly or they will start to collapse.

Baby Rolls in a Bun Tin

Try baking the rolls in a mini muffin tin. Unless you have two tins, you will need to do them in two batches: baking time is about the same as for the larger ones but keep an eye on them. These are great for children although the downside is, they disappear virtually as soon as they come out of the oven!

Baguettes

Again the recipe is the same as for the rolls and baps given previously. You can bake them on a large greased baking tray or you can buy special grooved and perforated trays to bake baguettes on: they usually hold three baguettes at a time.

When the dough is ready, put it onto a floured board and cut it into 4 pieces with a large knife. Turn each piece over so that the cut side is on top. Try to shape each one into a baguette shape while keeping the impression of the knife cut on top. Transfer them carefully to the prepared baking tray. Once the baguettes are baked, you will see how this makes them look really professional.

Bake in a preheated oven at 180–220°C (fan oven) or equivalent for 8–10 minutes until golden brown. Leave on the baking tray for a few moments and then remove and cool on a wire rack. A clean tea towel over the top will keep the baguettes fresh and moist as they cool.

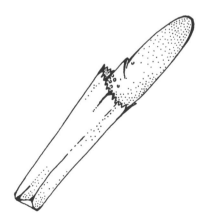

CURRANT BUNS

This is a useful recipe to have in your repertoire. You can leave out the spice and candied peel for a more everyday bun and use the full recipe to make your own hot cross buns at Easter time.

MAKES 12

450g (1lb) strong white
   bread flour
1 teaspoon mixed spice
   (optional)
1½ teaspoons quick yeast
1 teaspoon salt
25g (1oz) unrefined caster
   sugar
1 egg
210ml (8fl oz) warm water
2–3 tablespoons of mild
   oil
110g (4oz) currants,
   raisins, sultanas, mixed
25g (1oz) candied, not
   mixed, peel, diced
   (optional)

You will need a large
   greased baking tray

Put the flour and spice, if using, into the bread pan and the yeast, salt and sugar into separate corners on top. Add the egg, warm water and oil. Put into the machine: see below for the setting. Measure the dried fruit and candied peel, if using, and put it into the raisin compartment, if you have one: see below.

You will need to select the **raisin dough** setting. This means either the machine will beep after most of the kneading has been done, so you can rush to it at breakneck speed and add your dried fruit then, or, if you have a newer model, you will have put the fruit into a special compartment in the lid which will release it into the dough at the correct time. This is because if you add the fruit at the beginning it will be kneaded into an unappetising brown sludge with no discernible separate fruits!

Once the raisin dough programme has finished (usually around two hours and 20 minutes or so in most machines), take the dough out and put onto a lightly floured board. Divide into 12 pieces and lightly shape each piece into a ball and place on a greased baking tray. Alternatively, put each piece into the cups of a 12-cup muffin tin.

Cover lightly with greaseproof paper and leave in a warm place for about an hour or until the dough has just about doubled in size; that is to say, the size the finished buns will be.

Towards the end of this time, preheat the oven to 180–220ºC (fan oven) or equivalent.

Bake for 8–10 minutes or until golden brown. Remove from the oven and cool on a wire rack.

To make a sticky glaze

You can turn your buns into 'sticky buns' with this delicious easy glaze. Heat 2 tablespoons of caster sugar and 2 tablespoons of water together in a small heavy-bottomed pan until all the sugar is melted and bubbling. Brush the glaze over the buns and allow them to cool slightly before serving.

Make yourself a cup of tea and have a bun: you deserve it!

TEA CAKES

These are absolutely lovely eaten fresh with butter, although obviously the main idea is to have them split and toasted.

Put the yeast, sugar and salt into the bread pan and then add the flour and lard or vegetable shortening. Pour in the warm water.

Put the dried fruit into the raisin compartment and set the machine to the **raisin dough** programme.

Once the programme has finished put the dough onto a floured board and divide into 10 pieces. Shape into balls and flatten gently with your hands or a floured rolling pin. Space them out onto the greased baking tray(s), and leave to rise in a warm place for an hour or so until they have doubled in size.

Bake in a preheated oven at 180–220ºC (fan oven) or equivalent for 8–10 minutes until golden brown. Cool on a wire rack.

MAKES 10

1 teaspoon quick yeast
1 tablespoon sugar
1 teaspoon salt
450g (1lb) strong bread
   flour
35g (1½oz) lard or
   vegetable shortening
280ml (½ pint) warm
   water
110g (4oz) of mixed
   currants, raisins and
   sultanas

You will need 1 or 2
   greased baking trays

PANETTONE STYLE BUNS

*These little buns are based on the Italian Panettone. It's important to say that they are in the **style** of Panettone rather than **actual** Panettone: it is quite a long drawn out process to make the genuine article in Italy and involves a lot of skill and experience. Nevertheless, these are lovely and especially good dressed up at Christmas time with a dusting of icing sugar and a few ribbons. The muffin tin gives them just the right traditional shape.*

MAKES 12

½ teaspoon quick yeast
1 tablespoon unrefined
  caster sugar
1 teaspoon salt
300g (11oz) strong bread
  flour
140ml (scant ¼ pint) warm
  water
1 egg
1 egg yolk
1 teaspoon of vanilla extract
  or vanilla bean paste
Zest of 1 lemon
1–2 tablespoons mild oil
110g (4oz) raisins and
  sultanas, mixed
25g (1oz) candied peel,
  finely chopped

You will need a greased
  12-cup muffin tin

Put the yeast, sugar and salt into the bread pan and add the flour, warm water, egg, egg yolk, vanilla extract, lemon zest and oil. Put the dried fruit and candied peel into the raisin compartment and set the machine to raisin dough. Once the dough is ready, turn onto a floured board, divide into 12 pieces, shape gently into balls and put them into the prepared tin. Leave them in a warm place until they have doubled in size.

Bake in a preheated oven at 150ºC (fan oven) or equivalent for 7 minutes and then turn down the heat to 130ºC or equivalent, and bake for a further 3 minutes.

Remove from the oven and leave in the tin for a few moments then remove and cool on a wire rack. Dust with icing sugar.

PANETTONE STYLE CAKE

If you would like to try your hand at one large Panettone, put the mixture into a greased 18cm (7in) loose-bottomed cake tin and let it rise in a warm place until it has doubled in size and looks about the right size for the finished cake. Bake for 10 minutes at 150ºC and then turn the heat down to 130ºC and bake for a further 15 minutes. Leave to settle for a few moments then remove from the tin. Cool on a wire rack and dust with icing sugar.

Breakfast Buns

These taste a little bit like Danish pastries or those 'petits pains aux raisins' that are so lovely for a relaxing holiday breakfast with a cup of tea or coffee. The method for making these is very much simpler, though: it's done by making the dough very rich with extra butter and eggs.

Put the yeast, sugar and salt into separate corners of the bread pan and add the flour, butter, eggs, vanilla and water. Set the machine to the **dough** setting: usually about 45 minutes.

When the dough is almost ready put all the filling ingredients into a small saucepan and heat gently until the butter has melted, the sugar has dissolved and the fruit is plumping up a little.

The finished dough will be quite sticky so flour your hands before you take it out of the machine and keep the board and rolling pin lightly floured throughout. Once the dough is out of the machine, divide it into two pieces and roll them into two oblong shapes.

Cool the fruit and butter mixture and spread it down the centre of each of the two oblongs of dough, using the back of a dessertspoon to help you. Roll up each oblong like a Swiss roll and cut each one into 6 slices.

Use a fish slice to manoeuvre the buns onto the prepared baking tray, flatten each one very gently with your hand, and leave to prove a little for 10–20 minutes before baking. They need to be spaced out on the baking tray as they spread slightly.

Bake in a preheated oven at 180–220ºC (fan oven) or equivalent for approximately 8–10 minutes, until slightly puffed and golden. Remove from the tray with a broad palette knife or fish slice and cool on a wire rack.

These are great as they are, slightly warm, or you may like to drizzle them with a little **Lemon Glacé Icing** once they are cold. They are at their best eaten very fresh.

MAKES 12 buns

For the dough
½ teaspoon quick yeast
1 tablespoon unrefined
  caster sugar
1 teaspoon salt
250g (9oz) strong bread
  flour
50g (2oz) cold diced
  butter
1 egg
1 egg yolk
½ teaspoon vanilla extract
  or vanilla bean paste
130ml (4½fl oz) warm
  water

For the filling
110g (4oz) sultanas, raisins
  and currants, mixed
25g (1oz) butter
25g (1oz) soft brown
  sugar
½ teaspoon mixed spice

You will need a large
  greased baking tray

CHELSEA BUN TYPE VERSION

If you would like to make some buns with more of a Chelsea bun-like texture follow the recipe above, but increase the flour to 300g (11oz). This will make them less rich and more 'bunny'.

Traditionally, Chelsea buns huddle together as a joined batch in a baking tin, round or rectangular; you can bake them like this or on a baking tray. If you would like to bake them together in a tin choose either a 23cm (9in)round loose-bottomed cake tin or a 30 x 20cm (12 x 8in)rectangular roasting or baking tin.

HOME-MADE PIZZA

Home-made pizzas are hard to beat. It's easy to make your own dough by hand but even easier in a bread machine. One particularly welcome aspect of home-made pizzas is that you can have a fried egg on top if you like: hooray! It might be because they take virtually split-second timing to cook that you never seem to be offered them in pizza restaurants. Pizzas are great to eat outside in the garden in the summer but just a word of warning: if the weather is really hot and sultry forget about making your own base. It's exactly the same as with bread: the dough just goes all sloppy and sticky and totally unmanageable in the heat and humidity.

MAKES 2 x 20–23cm
  (8–9in) pizzas

½ teaspoon quick yeast
1 teaspoon salt
½ teaspoon sugar
300g (11oz) strong white
  bread flour
210ml (7fl oz) water
1–2 tablespoons mild oil

You will need 2 pizza pans,
  approximately 30cm
  (12in) in diameter or 2
  baking sheets, greased

Put the yeast, salt and sugar into the bread pan of your machine and put the flour on top. Pour in the warm water and the oil. Set the machine to **dough** programme: it should take about 45 minutes.

Once the dough is ready, turn it onto a lightly floured board and cut it into two. Flour your hands and roll the first piece into a ball and then flatten into a disc. Use a lightly floured rolling pin to help you.

The dough will be quite elastic and will keeping pinging back, but persevere. When you have got a fairly flat disc, lift it onto your rolling pin and transfer it to the pizza pan or tray. You might like to roll it a bit larger when it's on the tray: a child's rolling pin is ideal for this. Repeat with the second piece.

For the very best pizza bases, cover loosely with greaseproof paper and leave the dough to rise on the tray for about an hour in a warm place.

After about an hour, set the oven to a high setting, 220ºC (fan oven) or equivalent, and put on the topping of your choice.

Topping suggestions
1 quantity of **Easy Tomato Sauce for Pasta** (page 71), or a good-quality pasta sauce from a jar
Mozzarella cheese, drained of whey

Whatever else you fancy, such as:

• Sliced mushrooms • Sliced ham • Sliced salami or pepperoni • Anchovies • Olives •
Capers • Pineapple • Jalapeno peppers • Sliced red, green and yellow peppers •
Sliced chilli peppers • Egg (see below) • Freshly ground black pepper • Oregano, fresh or dried

Start with the tomato sauce; just spread it on quite thinly, you don't want too much. Arrange the rest of your chosen toppings over the sauce: if you are going to put an egg on top leave a clear space in the middle.

Baking time depends very much on your oven but, as a guide, bake for 10–12 minutes. If you are having an egg on top, bake for 7–8 minutes and remove carefully from the oven, closing the oven door immediately. Crack the egg in the middle of the pizza and return to the oven for 3–4 minutes.

Suggested topping combinations
Although you can go down the 'everything on it' route you might prefer slightly more themed toppings – Ham and Mushroom, Ham and Pineapple and so on – but if you want to go mad there is no reason why you shouldn't!

You can't go wrong with simple **Cheese and Tomato**. Spread the tomato sauce sparingly over the base and top with slices of mozzarella. Grind a little black pepper over the top. You could also use grated Cheddar instead of mozzarella.

Another great combination is **Pepperoni, Jalapeno and Fried Egg on a Wholemeal Base**. Make up the pizza dough with 250g (9oz) strong white flour and 50g (2oz) wholemeal flour.

Spread the base with tomato sauce and top with mozzarella. Arrange slices of pepperoni on top of that, leaving a clear space in the middle for the egg. Add a few sliced jalapeno peppers from a jar. Bake for 7–8 minutes, remove from the oven, crack your egg into the space in the middle and return to the oven for 3–4 minutes.

PIZZA PUTTANESCA

If you eat pizza a lot and feel like a change of topping, try this one based on the well-known pasta sauce.

1 red chilli

1 clove garlic

50g tin anchovy fillets in oil

400g tin of tomatoes

Roughly 75g (3oz) black pitted olives

1–2 teaspoons pickled capers, drained

Mozzarella cheese, drained of whey

Fry the chilli and garlic gently in oil from the anchovies. Snip half of the anchovy fillets into small pieces and add to the pan. Stir so that the anchovies break up completely and cook gently. Break up the tomatoes with a fork, remove any skin or central core and add to the pan. Chop half of the olives into small pieces and add to the pan with the capers. Stir everything together and simmer gently for half an hour or so.

When you are ready to bake the pizza, spread the topping over the base (don't feel you have to use it all; if you have any left over it will keep in the fridge for a couple of days, to use over pasta later). Slice some mozzarella over the top and arrange the rest of the olives and anchovies on top of that. Bake for 10–12 minutes.

INDEX